PUBERTY girl

Shushann Movsessian

ALLEN&UNWIN

To my mother Victoria Movsessian for having her periods. She created a lot of possibility.

First published in 2004

Allen & Unwin
83 Alexander Street
Crows Nest NSW 2065
Australia
Phone: (61 2) 8425 0100
Fax: (61 2) 9906 2218
Email: info@allenandunwin.com
Web: www.allenandunwin.com

National Library of Australia
Cataloguing-in-Publication entry:

Movsessian, Shushann.
Puberty girl.

1. Puberty. 2. Teenage girls - Growth.
3. Teenage girls - Health and hygiene. I. Title.

ISBN 978 1 74114 104 7.

Set in 10/15pt TheMix by Seymour Designs
Printed in China through Colorcraft Ltd., Hong Kong

7 8 9 10 11 12 13 14 15 **CC** 17 16 15 14 13 12 11 10 09

ACKNOWLEDGMENTS

When I think about the groups I've run over the past 13 years I'm touched and inspired by the thought that I've worked with around 1040 girls! It puts a smile on my face to think that some of these girls may be 25 years old now and may even have children of their own. Wow! All you Puberty Girls out there, thank you for challenging me with honest and difficult questions, being open and curious about growing up, sharing your stories, listening with compassion to each others' concerns and generally sharing your incredible and creative ideas, solutions and wisdom. This book would never have been possible without you.

I also feel blessed to know so many gorgeous women who have supported me along the way and shared generously of their stories. Many thanks to all you fabulous, intelligent, feisty, powerful, fun, creative, tender-hearted, strong-spirited women! The list is long and spans across continents. Specific thanks to the dynamic Lyn Clune who was there from the beginning and believed in the importance of this topic at the Royal Hospital for Women Randwick, Australia, Jane Svensson, for continuing to support these groups and my co-facilitator Marg Erwin. Thank you to Di Todaro and Liz Seymour at CKSD for their support and belief in the value of this book and to the team at Allen & Unwin. Thank you to all the Puberty Girls who gave us their valuable feedback: Thea Brash, Eliza Cavalletto, Sophie Marshall, Anna Phillips, Lucy Phillips and Carla Todaro. Thank you to all the Puberty Girls who supported us for our photoshoots: Jamie Ayoub, Eliza Cavalletto, Vanessa Harnn, Laura Lee McLaughlin, Davina Mahlsteadt, Isabella Mercuri, Bianca Mercuri, Jessica Pinker, Rachel Pinker, Anna Phillips, Lucy Phillips, Carla Todaro and M'Lisa Ward.

Finally thanks to my dear friends and colleagues for their enthusiasm, stories and support: Gemma Summers, Alexandra Pope, Sarah Parry, Jen Fox, Silvia Camastral, Amanda Frost and Anna Cole. You beauties! Your blood's worth bottling!

PETRI KURKAA

CONTENTS

INTRODUCTION
Welcome to puberty

Dear Puberty Girls

You are just about to step into one of the most incredible adventures of your life and all the possibilities that exist by simply being who you are and letting life happen! Congratulations!

Did you know that you're a walking, talking miracle? Well you are! Over the next few chapters of this book you're going to see exactly what I mean. Even while you're reading this there are a whole lot of changes happening—some of them you might be able to see, like maybe you're starting to get little breast buds, and some of them are inside you. You might feel them but can't see them.

Puberty means grown up or adult. Do I hear 'Ewww, gross!' out there? I know you aren't adults yet, but puberty is part of our growing process in becoming adults. If that sounds yucky or even scary let me say straight off that you're not alone. All your friends are probably going through the same or similar process and all the adults you know have also gone through this. Just imagine your big sister, mum, aunty or school teacher had to go through all the changes you are going through and maybe they were also thinking, 'grooosss, puberty no way!'. It's just that we don't really talk about it much with each other.

But for your information here are just a few people who have gone through the process of puberty: just think, Joan of Arc, Princess Diana and Cleopatra in one way or another went through the same journey you are going through. Can you imagine the queen, (none other than Elizabeth Regina) when she first started getting her periods? Or what about Britney? Even your gran! In fact, if your gran hadn't got her periods what do you think might have happened?

I like to call this the Puberty Girl Hall of Fame. You might want to add a few famous names yourself and, while you're at it, add your own!

What I really secretly wish for you reading this book is that you'll not only feel good about who you are, but that you'll feel Super-duper Fantastic, out there Fantabulous, Girl-power Wicked!

It is empowering to have the right information, to not have to hide who we are or feel embarrassed about it. It is empowering to learn about ourselves and to be ourselves, to be healthy, to feel good about who we are and to get as much support and encouragement and love as we can, because we deserve it!

So, in the adventure of this book we'll be looking, I mean *really* looking, at all the challenging, juicy, gooey, oozy, fuzzy, wuzzy, wild, private, personal parts of being a girl growing up. This includes changes to our body, our mind and thoughts and our feelings and emotions. There will be lots of opportunities for those really tough questions to be answered and the honest-to-goodness truth of what goes on in there, down there and around there! Finally, I do hope you enjoy this book and it helps you a little on your journey, and I especially hope you enjoy the journey of growing up into women.

Lotsa love, Shushann

P.S. Not everyone reading this book has a mum, sister or aunty to ask about all the goings-on of puberty. But you don't have to only talk to your family or caregiver. When I say mum or dad or aunty, think about any adult or older person in your life you trust and feel comfortable talking to. Think about who this could be for you, like a close friend, a teacher or school counsellor that you know and who cares about you.

chapter 1

Why a book on PUBERTY?

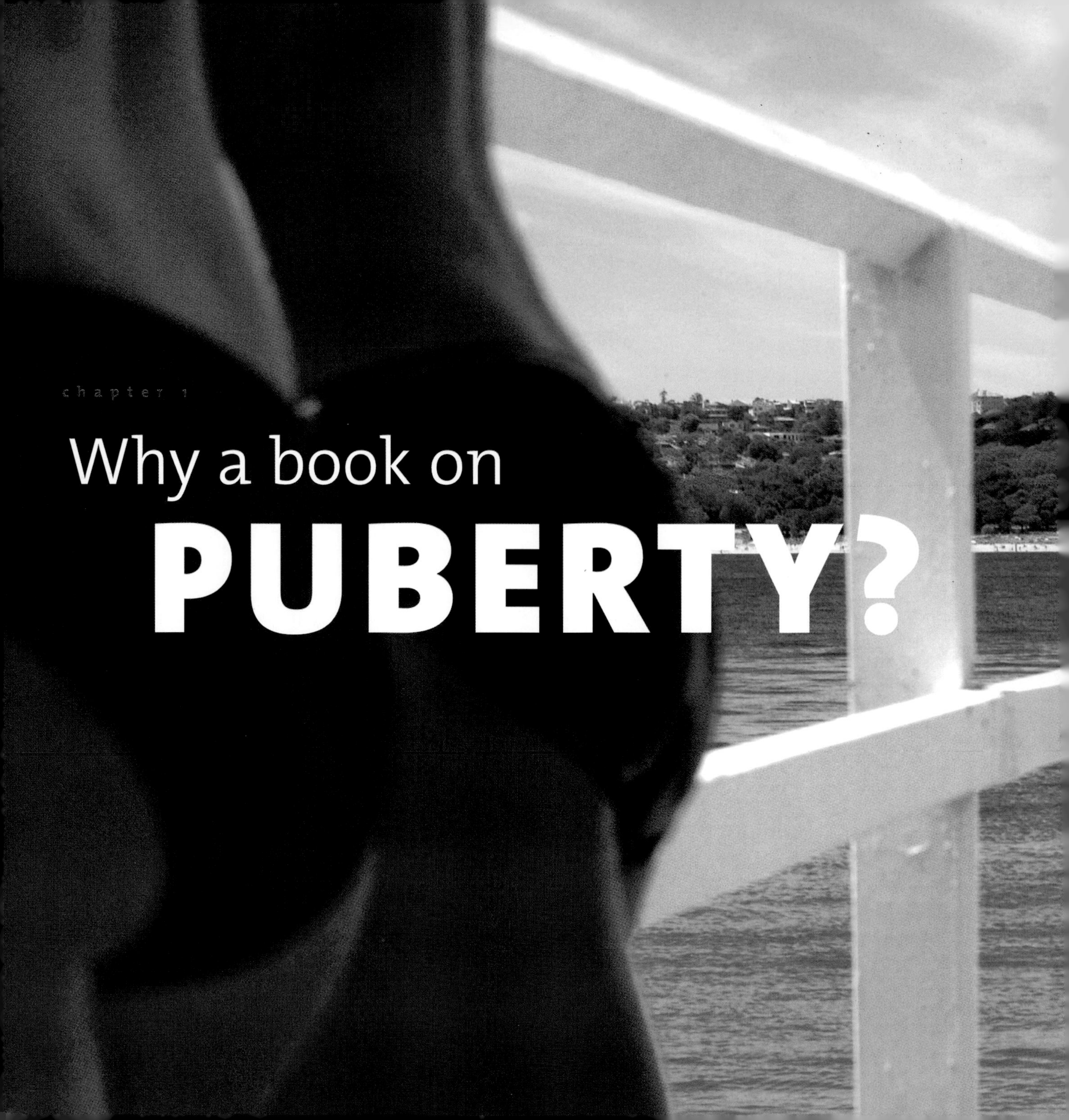

I've put this book together because over the last 13 years I've spoken to so many girls your age on puberty and growing up through groups that I've run. We have an action-packed day together where we talk, ask questions, get grossed out and laugh about all the changes that are happening to our bodies and emotions, from pimples to pubic hair, from teasing to our inner strengths and beauty. I've hung in for those 13 years because the strength, wisdom, beauty and creativity of the young girls I've worked with never ceases to amaze me. Usually the day starts with me asking, 'How many of you really didn't want to come today but came because mum or dad said so?' Of course nearly all the group puts up their hand—mostly because they feel uncomfortable, embarrassed and sad about having to grow up! (I told you, you weren't the only one!) By the end of the day this all changes; girls tell me how much more

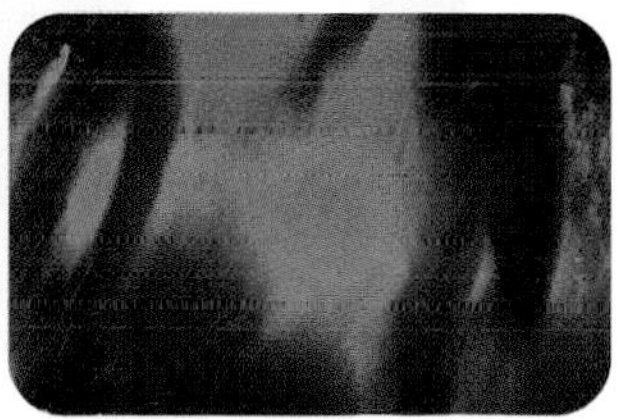

comfortable and prepared they feel, because we're all in it together and it's not as bad as they thought. Some (shock horror!) even say they're looking forward to growing up and becoming a woman. When I hear this I feel happy and proud. Like I've had a big slice of chocolate fudge cake with hot chocolate sauce and chocolate ice-cream! (You guessed it, I loooove chocolate!)

This book is hopefully a way of carrying the flame of the work I've been doing with Puberty Girls like you and maybe by the next few chapters in this book you may find that there are some big pluses + + + + to growing up and . . . look out—you might even be looking forward to your puberty! (Okay did I go too far? Or at least you'll be a little more prepared for it). Put it this way, you're probably in the middle of these

changes, there's no looking back now, so you may as well make the most of it! You might already know a little or even a lot about puberty and growing up from your parents or stuff at school. For starters, can you think of all the words that connect with the word 'Puberty'? You might want to try this with some of your friends. Write them all on a piece of paper. Go on, don't hold back, I want the juicy details and all the stuff you've heard.

Here are some of the words that girls in my groups have come up with:

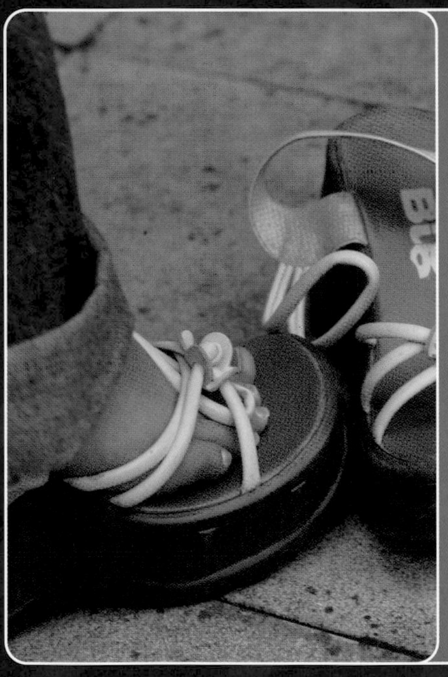

MENSTRUATION ❊ EMBARRASSING ❊ YUCKY! ❊ SMELLY ❊ SHAVING ❊ PERIODS ❊ RESPONSIBILITY ❊ PADS ❊ WAXING ❊ TAMPONS ❊ DEODORANT ❊ MOODY ❊ BREASTS ❊ TITS ❊ VAGINA (hair down there!) ❊ HOOTERS ❊ GRUMPY ❊ PENIS ❊ WEE HOLE ❊ WILLY ❊ DICK ❊ BRAS ❊ HAIRS ❊ UNDERARM HAIRS ❊ PUBIC HAIR ❊ BLOOD AND BLEEDING ❊ B.O. ❊ HAIRY LEGS! ❊ JUGS ❊ MAKE-UP ❊ GROWN UP ❊ BOYFRIENDS ❊ BABIES ❊ WET DREAMS ❊ PAIN ❊ EMOTIONS ❊ CRAMPS

Did you have some of these things in your list?

During this book we're going to talk more about some of these words and look at the pictures that go with them. We're also going to look at the proper words for some of what we've written. For example, do you know another word for periods?

The story of a Puberty Girl a little older than 10

I'm the first to admit that when I got my periods I felt EMBARRASSED, SCARED, CHEATED, CONFUSED, ANGRY, SHY, SAD, MOODY to name a few! Even though I was going on an adventure, it didn't really feel like it at the time. Mostly because I felt totally unprepared and alone. No-one had ever told me what to expect and what I could do about it and no-one talked about it. I thought I was the only one and I didn't want to change. Have you ever felt some of these feelings about puberty and getting the 'P' word (yep, your periods)?

That's partly why I've put a special section in this book called, 'Periods and puberty yuck!!!' because I've heard that so many times from girls in the groups I've run. I think I was even more mega-scared when I was growing up because no-one really told me what a period was. When I got them I thought I was sick or wounded or something dreadful. And then when I heard I was going to get it every month—'Ohhh, My God! No way!!' But, then I found out, 'Yes way!'

I'm happy now because I know that regularly getting my periods keeps me healthy. How? Well, because it means that all my growing up bits—my inner sexual organs—are working like they should be. But getting my periods also means that my bones and hair, nails and skin are also growing and healthy. I talk about this some more in my next chapter, it's called, 'Ooh la la: what's happening to me?' (You can turn to it now if you want to and have a sneak preview and check out some of the pictures.)

I got my first period when I was 9. This might sound young but the age range for girls getting their periods these days is actually between 9 and 15. Maybe there were other girls in my class who got their periods then too, but we never talked about that sort of stuff so I never got to know. Talking about your periods came under the 'that's way too embarrassing' category, but looking back it might have helped us feel a little more comfortable about ourselves if one of us was brave enough to speak up. Are you able to speak to your mum, dad or a close family member about your periods? Do you have at least one close friend you can trust to talk about your periods with?

When I was 9, I was a bit of a tomboy (well, I prefer tomgirl!). I was into athletics and other outdoorsy stuff. I have to say, I did notice some hairs starting to grow under my arms (which I called alfalfa sprouts), and that I was starting to get little titties, but I still didn't know that there was more to come in my body changes. There were … periods—eeek! It wasn't till I was about 14 or 15 that I started telling some of my friends that I had my period. That was usually to ask whether a friend had a pad or tampon and even then we'd use code and lower our voices to nearly a whisper.

Pads and tampons

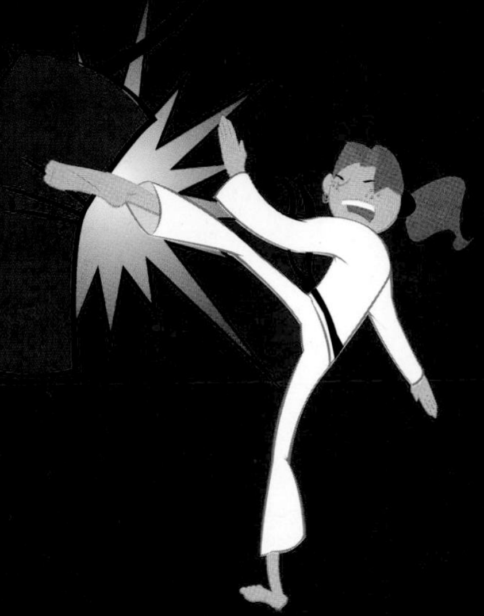

When I first got my periods I started to wear pads to school—oh, them pads, them pads, them white pads. They were huge white rectangles and we'd wear them with an elastic belt that had clips on each end to hold them in place. You can forget your ultra-thin, super-adhesive minis with wings! If you saw them you'd really understand why we called them surfboards. Really!

When I first wore them, I felt like I was wearing a sandwich in my knickers. Because I had to attach them with an elastic belt that had a clip on each end, by the time I'd got off the school bus and walked into the school, the pad had gradually slipped around and ended up somewhere in the middle of my back, giving me this strange looking lump. How embarrassing! Something like Connie the Camel! Not a good look, especially when you have to walk past that really cute guy at the bus stop.

So, I would try and be cool and pretend everything was absolutely normal, yep, everything's normal, I just have this strange lump on my back, so what, doesn't everyone? I'd madly race into the toilets and move the pad down. I remember our sixth grade teacher telling us about puberty and getting our periods. She said: 'Girls, one day a basket will grow inside of you and this basket is preparing for you to have a baby.'

Oh, plleeasse! A basket? Well I think by the end of her 'basket' talk we were all turning into basket cases! And we had no idea that what she was trying to describe was our **uterus** (heard that word before? No? well you'll hear about it again very soon) and getting our periods. Ahhh, thank goodness for growing up.

Well there's no doubt about it, I did get my periods, and once I had a regular period I would get it for about the same amount of days every month. You could have blown me down with a feather if you had said to me when I was 9 or 10 that I'd be running groups on puberty or even writing a book about it! So here I am. Sure as eggs is eggs (or should I say ovaries is ovaries!!), you're growing up too. Look where growing up has got you so far—your own teeth, you can actually walk, talk, go to the toilet by yourself and you can use the internet (ahem, with permission of course!).

Here is a conversation that might be had in a quiet corner in the girls' toilets:

Girl A (with period): Hey, (cough, cough) ummm I've run out of surfboards (name used for sanitary pads). I don't suppose you've got one I could borrow?

Girl B: Borrow?? I don't want you giving it back to me after you've used it!

Girl A: Shhh, no, no, I mean do you have a spare one.

Girl B: No sorry, I haven't got any surfboards, but what about a mintie (word used for tampons)? I've got some of those.

Girl A: Oh, okay, yeah that'll do, thanks.

Did you know . . .
Menstruation comes from the Latin word **menses** meaning monthly. That's 'cause girls and women get their periods about once a month.

According to astrologists, most girls' periods fall on the same cycle of the moon as when they were born.

Even as you read the next line on this page and take your next breath you're changing, growing and becoming the full dynamic potential of the wonderful self that you are . . . oops, you've just grown a little more, just then, when you blinked.

Writing in your diary/journal

Do you keep a journal? This is something where you can write your feelings, thoughts and ideas and is really meant for your eyes only. It's like having your own personal, private, bestest friend—you!

Take the opportunity to write down all your thoughts and feelings after reading each chapter. What you do with this is up to you. You might want to keep them totally private for yourself or you might want to share and talk about some of the stuff you've written with mum or a friend you feel close to and trust.

Try this simple exercise:

Write for 5+ minutes non-stop, without thinking too hard, on all the feelings and thoughts you have about getting your first period. Or, if you've already got your period, all the things you felt and thought about getting it. A good time to do this is when you wake up in the morning and are in that sleepy morning state. You could also do this with a friend—sharing what you've written is optional.

Menstrual myths: The good, the bad and the bleeding ugly truth

See how you go: TRUE OR FALSE?

- People will be able to notice when I have my periods.
- It's not okay to have a shower when I'm menstruating.
- It's okay for boys to know all about menstruation.

- When I have my periods I should avoid physical exercise.
- When I'm menstruating I can still go swimming.
- I should eat more meat when I start menstruating to get the right vitamins.
- When I have my periods I should keep it a secret and not tell anyone.
- Menstrual blood is dirty.
- I shouldn't wash my hair when I have my periods.
- I'll lose a lot of blood each month when I get my periods.

(Answers are on page 8)

Menstrual myths can bring a girl down

From what I've read, menstruation went down like a wet sanitary pad on a hot day in western history. Most old medical and religious writings on menstruation talked about it as shameful, unclean or unhealthy. No wonder you millennium gals say you feel uncomfortable or yucky about it. We've had generations of getting bad press about something as natural as having a period! Ancient Greek and Roman writers described menstrual blood as powerful and unclean (well I like the powerful part). I am amazed at how many girls think that menstrual blood is dirty, when in fact it's the cleanest most nourishing blood because it is where a baby grows.

Most of the bad stuff was written by men, and guess what? Men don't have periods. Maybe that's why they were so freaked out about it and had to put it down because it seemed strange, not normal and even scary to them; if they didn't get it then it must not be normal. They searched for the reasons women bled. Some of the beliefs floating around were:

1. There had to be something inferior about the way women are put together. (A tad confusing, I must say, considering we're painted over and over again by all the famous artists in history and these days we're plastered on just about every billboard!)

2. Women bled because they were cursed by God. Oh! Isn't that how a lot of prejudice starts—around difference and not understanding or respecting difference?
3. Women just had too much blood, so some of it had to come out monthly.
4. Others thought women menstruated because they didn't exercise or get out of the house as much as men did.
5. They thought the blood came out of the womb (uterus) because the womb was considered the weakest organ in the body, so it was the place the blood was most attracted to, like a hole in a bucket.
6. At one point they thought the womb could move around inside the body, even go up a woman's throat, and cause all sorts of strange medical problems. This was known as the 'wandering womb'. (Sounds like they had a case of the 'wandering brain' which it seems went missing on these occasions.)

These strange stories go on up to the present day. As late as the 1960s, medical guide books suggested that women should not take baths or exercise during their periods. If menstruation has always been feared or misunderstood, how do we learn to feel good about our bodies when we bleed? Well for starters read this book! And get the right info and speak out for being respected as growing girls/women and potential mothers.

So in answer to these myths that on the whole put down women and their bodies, maybe we Puberty Girls need to start challenging the myths, setting the story straight and standing with dignity for the incredible walking miracles that we are.

> 'I'm kind of scared and excited. Knowing that I'm growing up and that I can make my own decisions about life, like work and what's going to happen, who I want to be with and accept that I'm not a child any more.' Patty, 11

Answers

- No-one can tell you have your period unless you tell them!
- It's okay to bathe and swim when you have your periods. You may get some blood in the bath and you should wear a tampon if you swim.
- Of course it's okay for boys to know about menstruation—it's a natural part of life!
- You should do exercise all the time—having your period is no excuse.
- You don't need to eat more meat around your period; just make sure you're eating the right amounts all the time.
- It's okay to talk about your periods if you want to and if the person wants to listen!
- Period blood is clean. In fact, it's the cleanest you can get.
- You can wash any part of your body when you have your period.
- You'll only lose about 3 tablespoons of blood—and it's blood that's meant to be lost!

chapter 2

OOH LA LA

what's happening to me?

Girls usually start puberty before boys. We tend to start between ages 9 and 15, whereas boys come into puberty between 11 and 16 (and don't worry, plenty happens to them too).

Getting to know your body

As a first step towards understanding what happens during puberty, I want you to take a good look at your body. Go somewhere in your home where you feel safe and private and get naked. Eeek! Naked? Yes, you read right. Get to know your body. It's yours to look at. I'm not saying you do this in the middle of the kitchen while everyone's having dinner. I'm suggesting you do this somewhere you feel safe and free from any disturbances or interruptions, where you can lock the door so no-one can come barging in (especially your little sister or brother who always wants to know what's going on when the door's shut). You might want to do it after you've had a bath or a shower so you can look in the bathroom mirror. You might surprise yourself with what you see. For example, you might notice soft fine hairs growing around your pubic area or that your hips are getting more curvy.

You're going to need a hand-held mirror for this next part so that you can really take a close look. Go on, don't be shy. It's only you who's looking. It's easier if you can put a leg up on the bath for balance or squat in front of a hand-held mirror. What you see there is otherwise known as your **vulva**.

Did you know?

In the 1840s the average age for girls to start their periods was 16½. Today it's 12. This may be because our diets are now better and we're more aware of hygiene, which keeps us healthy and helps us develop earlier in age.

The changes to our bodies develop gradually, usually over several years, which gives us time to get used to our more adult body. Just as well—can you imagine waking up one morning and suddenly having boobs! Oops!

Do you know how many holes or openings you have front and back between your legs? Is it: A) 1 B) 4 C) 3 D) 2 E) 6

If you answered E) 6—eeek, that's way too many!
If you answered A) What, 1 for everything???
If you answered C) you're right, 3. That's just right for all our business.

Introducing without further ado, the three magic holes!

Weeell, they're not exactly magic but a lot of important stuff happens down there, you know! Firstly, you have an opening to your **urethra**, where your urine or wee comes out. You have an opening to your **anus** where your faeces or poo comes out, and in the middle of these two is your **vagina** where blood comes out when you've got your period and possibly a baby will come out of some time in the future.

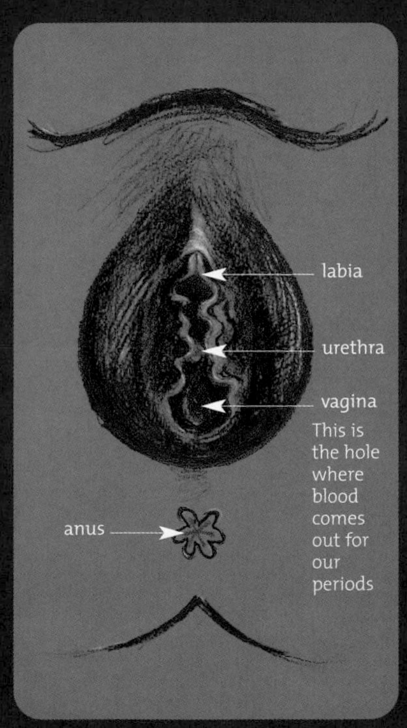

Vulva

That whole area between your legs is known as the vulva. I guess it's a lot easier than having to say 'that whole area between your legs' all the time. Please don't confuse this with Volvo which is something your parents might drive you to school in—it could be a little embarrassing to mix the two names up in public.

Vulva comes from the Latin word volva, which means covering.

The Indian Sanskrit word *yoni* translates to 'vulva' but it has also been used to describe the vagina. This ancient feminine symbol was worshipped for its fertility and source of all life. It was also seen as powerful and creative. I can just hear you now, 'Yep, that's me! I'm just one big, walking, talking ball of power and creativity!'

If you haven't totally fainted or aren't grossed out by now and are still looking at your magic holes with your hand-held mirror, you'll see that your vulva has soft folds of skin which cover the urethra and the vagina and the clitoris. These folds are known as the **labia** (Latin for lips). There are two lots of lips: **labia majora** (big lips) for the larger outer folds of skin, and **labia minora** (little lips) for the smaller inner folds. They gradually become more distinct and developed as we grow.

Why do we have these lips? Well, they are important because they provide a protective covering for our vagina against dirt or germs that might enter our vaginal opening; they protect us against bacterial infection when we have our periods; and they form a soft protection to the vaginal opening when we are pregnant. So, there you are, safe for us and safe for a possible baby coming through.

The clitoris—or the jewel in the crown

Slightly peaking through the top of where our labia minora (little lips) meet at the top of our vulva is a small, super-sensitive organ known as the **clitoris**. It is about the size of a pea. Over the ages it's been called some cute names like the 'jewel in the crown'—maybe because it's at the crown of the vulva and once we've found it, we can't go past it. It's such a definitely pleasurable feeling to touch it. We may have met it by accident while washing ourselves in the bath. Or … we may have already explored our bodies and have known it's there for some time.

When I describe the clitoris to girls in my groups the ones who've been there, done that, are just nodding knowingly. They're like '. . . mm hmm, yep I know I've got one for sure, so what else is new?!' And then there are the ones that are looking at me like I've described how to speak Swahili underwater!

If you don't know what I'm talking about then this is where squatting in front of a mirror in the bathroom or your bedroom can be very, very helpful. I've included an illustration on page 16, but it's always better to look at the real thing, especially as part of getting to know your body.

You know you've found your clitoris because it is really sensitive, even tickly to touch. That's because it's got lots of nerve endings in it. Touching or rubbing our clitoris or around it can make us feel excited and melty inside. It's known as our very own pleasure spot. And giving ourselves this pleasure is also known as masturbating. This can happen at any age, children can do this as a way of comforting themselves at nap time sometimes. Touching ourselves in this way is a safe and private way to give ourselves pleasure.

V is for victory! It's also for vagina!

Why is it so hard to say this word? In my puberty groups girls can barely whisper it without falling about in hysterical laughter or falling into stunned silence. Well, I say vagina, vagina, vagina! Call it from the rooftops. We need it. Most of us came out of it and we wouldn't be here without it! Girls, love your vaginas!

You might have heard a lot of different names for the vagina. That could be why we can have a hard time saying the V word. Ooh, yes, there have been some pretty interesting names for the vagina over history, probably because people haven't been able to say vagina. Check out the list on the next page and see if you know of any that I've missed.

Our vagina is the hole or opening that connects our outer body to our inner body.

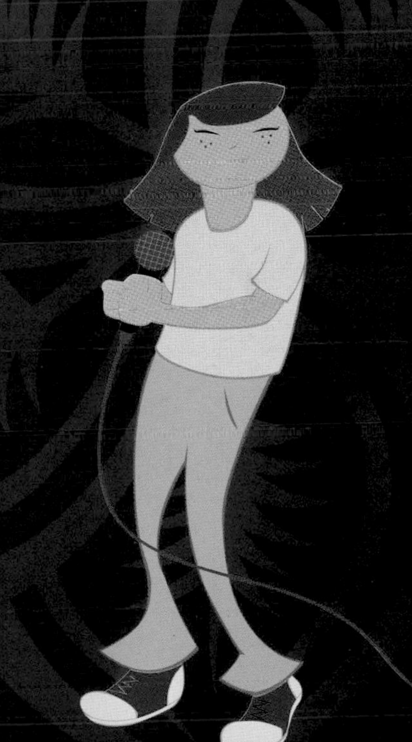

It's made from strong, stretchy muscle which eventually has to stretch to about 10 cm for a baby's head to push out through it. Ouch! Too much information?

The hole that we can see from the outside leads to the vaginal passage that leads into our **cervix**, which is the neck of our **uterus**, and the uterus is where a foetus grows into a baby and where blood, lining and tissue come out each month in our periods.

Now you know all the technical terms, let's look at some of the changes that might be happening to your body during puberty. I've called these **signposts** because some of them you may have recognised already. They are all indications that puberty and menstruation are about to happen.

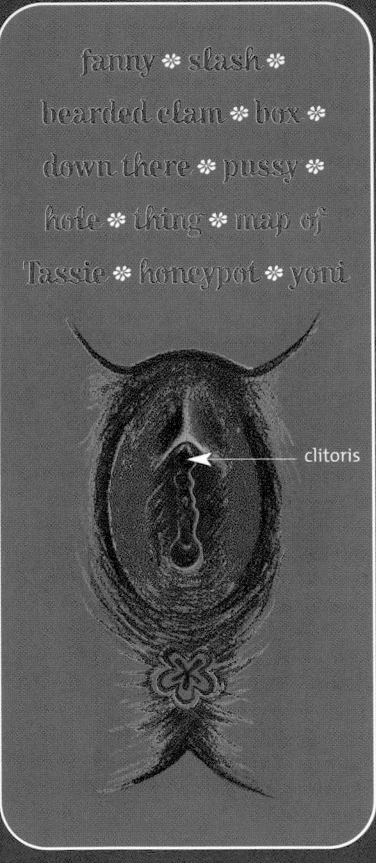

fanny ❀ slash ❀
bearded clam ❀ box ❀
down there ❀ pussy ❀
hole ❀ thing ❀ map of
Tassie ❀ honeypot ❀ yoni
clitoris

Did you know?

Signposts for the Puberty Girl

Have you noticed any of the following things?

1. Skin and hair starting to get more oily

Getting some tiny (or not so tiny) pimples on our face? These can usually appear around our forehead, nose and chin—otherwise known as our **t-zone**.

2. Getting taller and starting to gain weight— e.g. hips growing wider and body becoming more curvy

This is one of the first things you may be noticing about yourself around puberty. You're getting taller, but in particular you're gaining weight. Generally we gain about 1–2 kilos around our middle before puberty. But wait, we can gain up to 10 kilos in the 6 months before and after our puberty. This tends to be in the thigh, hip, boob and bottom areas, otherwise known as our **sex hormone-dependent areas**. Are you wondering 'But, but why couldn't we just get fat toes or fatter ears?!' Just remember, your body is going through major internal changes and these are having an effect on how we look externally. If it's any comfort, all girls go through the same deal.

Yes, yes, it's trrrruue!!! You may be screaming 'Why, why, why??' So sit down and I'll tell you. This is because we have an increase in appetite (i.e. Ai Carumba! We could eat a horse!) and a slowing down of our growth in height. There is a reason to all this madness—our body is stocking up its storeroom, getting ready for menstruation or getting our periods.

In a nutshell, the male sex hormone, **testosterone**, encourages fat loss and building muscle for boys and the female sex hormones, **oestrogen** and **progesterone**, increase fat levels and not so much muscle growth for girls.

Well, that's nature for you. Getting more curves is nature's way of preparing our bodies for possible babies; it loves women to be curvy. I'm giving you the bad news first so we get it out of the way—just like that sticky little band-aid, let's rip it off nice and quickly and it's over with—because there is good news too. But first let's clear up any questions about **puppy fat**.

And they call it PUPPY FAT

If you don't want to get puppy fat, then for starters don't feed your dog so much (hee hee)! I get asked a lot about puppy fat and it's always tricky giving a straight answer. How can I say this with tact—girls, unfortunately puppy fat is a bit of a myth. A lot of it is plain old

What's your exercise of choice?

Tap ✻ salsa ✻ jazz ✻ ballet (or your dance of choice!) ✻ gymnastics ✻ soccer ✻ aerobics ✻ footy ✻ yoga ✻ softball ✻ basketball ✻ tae kwon do ✻ karate ✻ walking ✻ jogging ✻ taking the dog for a walk ✻ Add your own if I've left something out.

overeating with no exercise, and it doesn't help when we're gaining some extra weight around our SHDA (sex hormone-dependent areas) during puberty. The message is eat healthy, keep the greasy, sugary foods to a minimum, keep up the exercise and you won't turn into a Teletubby!

Put some cha in your cha cha cha!

If you're already exercising, eating healthy (i.e. lots of fruit and vegies, not chocolate cake) and keeping fit then you're on the right track. We all need to do some exercise every day. That's going to change that fat we're so good at storing into muscle! So do whatever you do to put a spring in your step.

3. Growing pains—hands and feet getting larger

Hmmm . . . those mysterious growing pains that disappear just as quickly as they appear and then appear again somewhere else!

Growing pains can happen over two stages of our growth. The first is in our early childhood from 3–5 years old and the second is later around the time of our puberty at 8–12 years old. It's not really clear what causes this. It's not really bone pain and from what I know the discomfort doesn't last long. On the whole we grow in height first and strength later. We haven't quite built the muscles to support our growing bones.

Our feet and hands may grow bigger earlier at puberty because that's just the sequence of things. Some bits of us grow faster than others. The lengthening of our facial features happens later and the final lengthening happens in our spines. That's why you might see some teens who seem to have short bodies but these really big feet. Don't worry, it all catches up to itself in the end. Just think of yourself as a bit of a caterpillar, munching your way through puberty, stocking up in preparation to come out as that dazzling butterfly!

'You become independent. You learn to live your own life.

You get to earn your own money and buy your own place.' Tamara, 10

4. More fatty tissue in breasts—little buds start to form and nipples get a little darker than the outer area of the breasts

Once you start getting underarm hair you will probably also notice that your breasts begin to form little buds. Sounds cute. Little breast buds, like flowers. These are little fatty lumps under the nipples and they may even be slightly tender. The nipple, and the area around the nipple, called the **areola**, will also get a little darker and stand out more. This happens because eventually a baby's mouth will need to get round it to suckle for milk. All mammals have breasts and humans are no exception. Breasts, which are milk-producing glands, begin to enlarge in females around puberty. They're made of fat and other tissue that surrounds and protects nerves, blood vessels and milk ducts (small tube-like paths).

The time your breasts start to develop varies from girl to girl. Some girls start getting breasts at 8, other girls start at 14. It usually takes about 4 to 5 years for your breasts to reach an adult size.

Guys might tease you about breasts but it's common for them to develop a small amount of breast enlargement too. During puberty, hormones in the body cause the breasts to grow larger. The difference is that for guys this is usually temporary.

Breasts are wondrous things! Artists, sculptors, movie makers and songwriters have been fascinated by them for a very long time. If you're wondering about how your breasts might turn out, I suggest checking

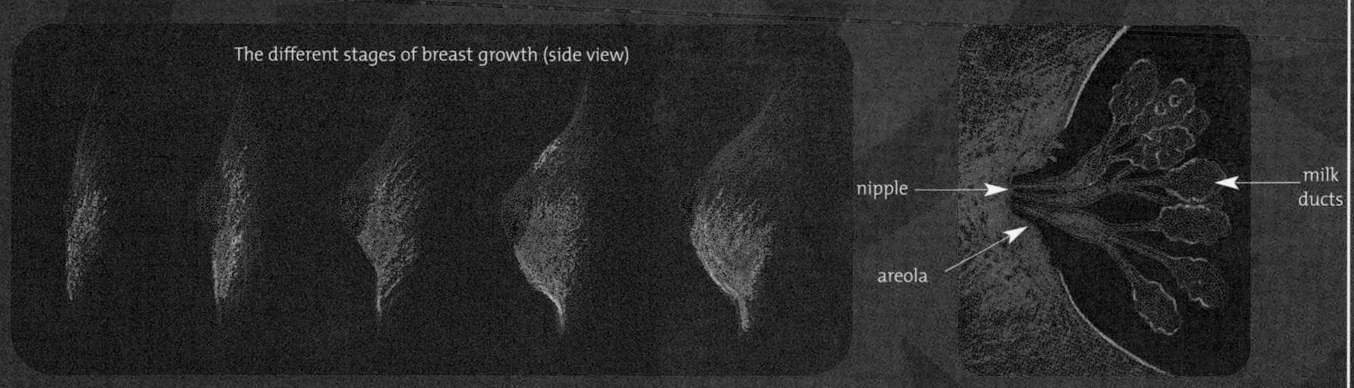

The different stages of breast growth (side view)

out mum's, Aunty Jean's or grandma's, to get an idea of the shape and size that yours might be. Try and do it in a way that doesn't look obvious, like with your mouth open and your eyes rolling around like you've choked on something!

Your ABC and D's about BRAS— sometimes known as 'over the shoulder boulder holders!'

Breasts come in all shapes and sizes and so there are bra sizes that are made to fit the width of your back (the number on the label) and the size of your breast (otherwise known as your cup size and they come in A, B, C or D). Believe it or not my gran was a double D—guess who I inherited my boobs from!?!

When I developed breasts at around age 11, I had a major case of rounded shoulders from all the slouching I did trying to hide that I had boobs. Much to my annoyance I had the 'juicy, juicy, mango' type of boob, compared to the 'juicy, juicy, cherry' type of boob. I was jealous of girls with small boobs who could walk around wearing a t-shirt or a singlet without having to wear a bra. I was sooooo embarrassed. What I didn't know till later was that my girlfriends with the small titties were dying to have bigger ones. When they'd go out they'd stuff tissues in their bras to make their boobs look bigger. What I learnt was that guys liked me for being cool with who I was on the inside rather than trying to fit some sort of image (well, the guys who were worth getting to know anyhow!). It took me years to walk around with my shoulders back and not feel embarrassed with how I looked. I hope it's sooner for you if not already. See my chapter on 'Your body means business' about feeling good about our bodies.

The craziest boob apparel I ever saw was when one of my teachers turned up to school in a top that was a little see-through and she'd put band-aids over her nipples instead of wearing a bra! Ai Carumba! I got a crick in my neck from doing a double take. Shame they didn't have crop

Ahh, the humble breast— it has collected quite a few names over the years. Here's a few you might come across by the time your buds become blossoms!

Jugs or Milk Jugs · Hooters · Tits · Titties · Boozies · Headlights · Boobs · Gazongas! · Melons · Juicy Mangoes

You could make up your own names or do what I do and call them breasts.

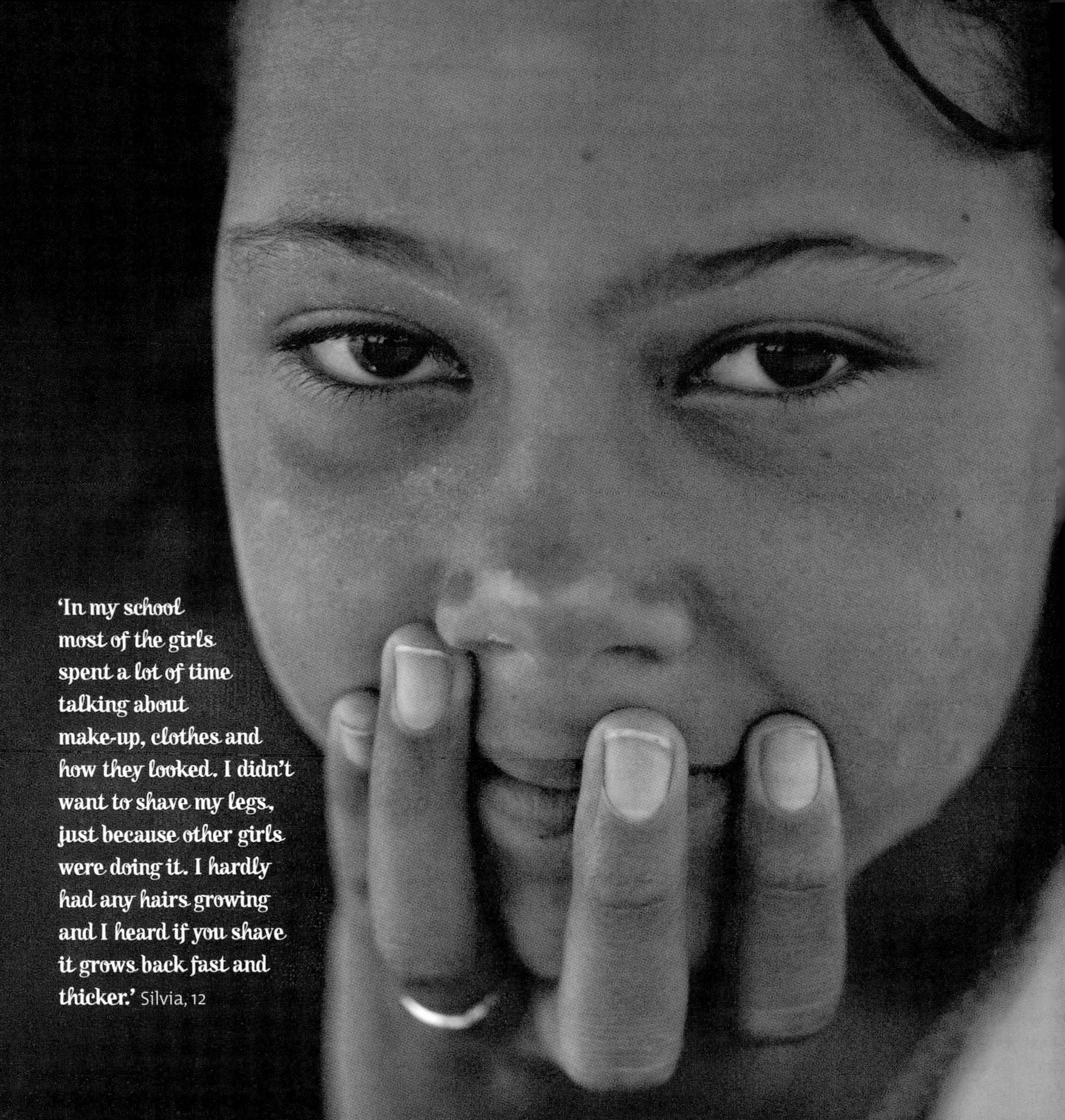

'In my school most of the girls spent a lot of time talking about make-up, clothes and how they looked. I didn't want to shave my legs, just because other girls were doing it. I hardly had any hairs growing and I heard if you shave it grows back fast and thicker.' Silvia, 12

tops in those days because that would have been a good option for this teacher. Crop tops and sports tops are great when you're starting off.

Training bras

Some girls get training bras around the time of their puberty. They're like a boob version of training wheels until you move up into serious boob apparel and there's plenty around! If you are serious about getting a properly fitted bra and aren't sure what your breast size is you can get yourself measured for a free fitting in a bra shop or at a large department store. This is done with a trained bra fitter who is usually a woman. She'll measure your chest under your breasts to get the right bra size to fit across your back. Then she'll measure for the size of your cup, whether it's an A, B, C or D. She does this by measuring across your breasts where your nipples are.

Based on these measurements she'll make some suggestions about the sort of styles or brands you might want to try. There is an incredible variety of 'underwear candy' out there if you haven't already seen it when shopping with mum. It's like a bra bistro and manufacturers are coming up with more and more ideas to either make your boobs look smaller or bigger and then all the frou-frou that goes with that. Oh well, I guess that's better than the good ole, bad ole days of slouching or stuffing tissues in your bra, although tissues are a lot cheaper.

5. Here a hair, there a hair, everywhere a hair hair: hair on our legs getting a little thicker; starting to grow hair under our arms; growing pubic hair

About 6 months after your breasts start to develop, pubic hair may start to grow around your vagina or genital area. These are commonly known as your **pubes**. Sometimes these changes are happening so slowly that we hardly even notice them. These will start off being really soft and

The stages of pubic hair growth

before pubic hair growth

soft, downy hair

hair becoming thicker

more pubic hair growth

full pubic hair growth

Although these signposts indicate that your body is getting ready for the big day, it really is hard to pinpoint exactly when you will get your first period. It's like asking when exactly will trees start shedding their leaves for autumn? Or when exactly will a butterfly come out of its chrysalis? It is different for each of us because we're all gorgeously unique. Part of this process will depend on our height and body weight, since our bodies are such clever machines and we need to have just the right conditions for our periods to start. All you can do is prepare yourself by getting as much information as possible and watching out for some of these signposts.

downy and will gradually become thicker and for some people, very curly. These curly pubic hairs provide soft, bouncy protection around our sensitive vulva and vagina.

Similarly, if you lift up your arm and take a look underneath you'll notice that the skin under there connects to our breast tissue. The hair growing there is a form of protection for that delicate area surrounding our breast. This is particularly when our breasts might get more tender around the time of our period or when women are breastfeeding.

The hairs under our arms and pubes are probably leftovers from prehistoric times when our whole bodies were covered in hair. I guess that's before underarm waxing was invented. Having said that, you may want to consider your options—waxing, shaving or simply going a la naturale. That will be your personal choice. Although your underarms may get a little sweaty with hairs, they aren't any more or less smelly without them—and remember, there's always soap and deodorant.

Last signpost . . . some sticky, pale yellowish mucus in your panties

This is called **show** and is one of the last signs of your body's changes before you get your first period. You can usually expect to get your period about 6 months after you have your first **show**. But don't worry if you don't, it can really vary—we're all different . . .

The nitty, sticky thing about mucus is that it's a liquid, sometimes pasty secretion that is not only present in our vaginas, but in other parts of our bodies, e.g. the runny stuff in our noses can be described as mucus. It helps lubricate things. Yeah, yeah, I know, I'm getting yucky again.

The mucus in our vaginas actually comes from the lining of our uterus or womb. It is wet because it has water in it, amongst other things. Mucus constantly changes its thickness and appearance during the menstrual cycle—sometimes it can be thin, clear and runny and look a little like when you've blown your nose and other times it's more thick and white and looks pasty. The female hormone progesterone controls what it does and how it looks. I talk more about why we have mucus and hormones in my next chapter, 'The big M'.

If you've noticed some or any of these changes . . . CONGRATULATIONS . . . you are on the road to being a Puberty Girl!

I remember being really surprised when I noticed I had some soft hairs sprouting under my arms while taking a shower shortly before I got my periods. I just looked down and . . . What!? . . . Where did they come from?

Sarah, 12

Girls, when in doubt, blame it on the hormones. I'm in a bad mood? It's the hormones. I want to eat that big slab of chocolate cake? It's the hormones. I've just got more hair on my body? It's the hormones. I'm getting oilier skin, hair and pimples? But of course, all together now, 'It's the hormones!'. They can do some funny things to our bodies, they can. You may start off being a mild-mannered little girl, minding your own business, getting on with things and then what happens? You fill out, get hairs growing all over the shop, get boobs and you become . . . 'PUBERTY GIRL!'

chapter 3

the big M

No, I'm not talking about McDonald's, I'm talking about the other big M—**menstruation**—another word for periods. You might have an idea yourself from school but here is some information to set the story straight. Our bodies go through cycles in much the same way as nature does—day to night, new moon to full moon, spring through to winter. Our bodies have cycles for digestion, for nails and hair to grow, and of course the monthly cycle of our menstruation.

Our menstrual cycle is like most of nature's cycles: something new starts to form, it grows to maturity and then gradually starts to die, so that it can start all over again. We talked in Chapter 2 about some of the changes that we may notice on the outside. Our menstrual cycle involves a lot of changes happening on the inside to our sexual reproductive organs. This cycle usually takes a period of between 25–35 days and that's why it's often called our period.

The Curse! ❀
That time of the month
❀ Monthlys ❀
The 'Happy Event' ❀
My things ❀ It ❀

Ye olde words for periods

There are lots of crazy and creative words for our periods. We never really used the word periods or menstruation in the playground when I was growing up. To the right are some words which were part of the code we used so that people wouldn't know what we were talking about—especially if there were boys around! I've added a few more that I've picked up along the years.

The step-by-step lowdown on the menstrual cycle

When our bodies are ready to start a menstrual cycle our brain sends a message to our reproductive organs via a little gland called the **pituitary gland**. The pituitary gland sits at the base of our brain and up a little. If we had superwomen X-ray vision and could look inside our bodies at our reproductive or inner sex organs, we'd see that we have two glands called **ovaries**, one on each side of our pelvis, two **Fallopian tubes**, and a

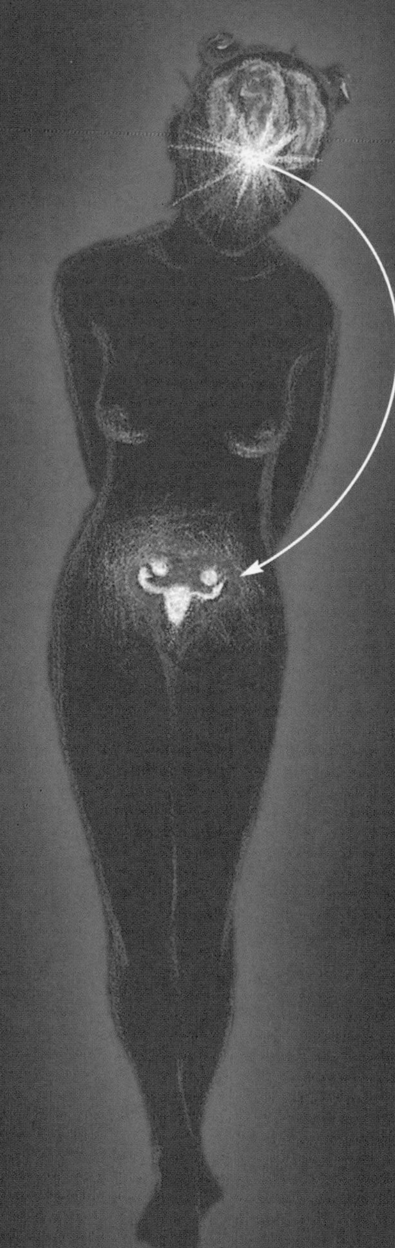
The brain sends a message to the ovaries to produce an egg when the time is right.

cervix which leads into a hollow muscle called our uterus.

All this is packaged very neatly. If you place your index fingers down where your legs meet your body so that they're touching, and opened your thumbs out to form a little triangle, you'll find your uterus. Check it out on yourself. Yep, all in that little space.

When the timing is right for our body to start a period, then the pituitary gland in our brain starts up a conversation with our sex organs. This is through chemical messengers in our blood called **hormones**. The two main hormones for girls are **oestrogen** (pronounced east-ro-jen) and **progesterone** (pronounced pro-jester-own). Here is how that conversation more or less goes:

1. '**Brain to ovary, brain to ovary, do you read me? Time to grow an egg**'. Using the hormone oestrogen the brain sends a message to one of the ovaries to grow an egg (or **ovum**). In response, the ovary starts to grow about 10 to 20 eggs (**ova**) which start to get bigger through the stimulation of the hormone oestrogen.
2. '**Ovary to uterus, grow some lining and make it soft, just in case . . .**' The ovary also sends a message to the uterus to grow a lining through the hormone progesterone. If you make a fist in front of you, you'll get a reasonable idea of the size of your uterus (or womb, as they said in the old days) right now. It is a strong, stretchy muscle that's hollow inside and connects to your cervix which connects to your vagina. It's hollow because it's the space where a fertilised egg may grow into a foetus and eventually into a baby.

   This lining of the uterus is made up of tissue, mucus and blood and can be up to 1 cm thick. This is in preparation in case a baby should grow there. When there is no baby, the lining comes away naturally and makes up the blood we see when we have a period. Mucus is similar to the sticky liquid you might find when you blow your nose. Ewww, gross! But we'd be in trouble if we didn't have it because it acts as a soft, protective lubricant.

3. **'Ovary to brain, egg has grown and is ready waiting for your instruction, over.'** When one egg or ovum has grown large enough the ovary lets the brain know about it. By this stage the lining formed in the uterus is ready for a possible fertilised or non-fertilised egg that dies away and becomes part of our period. But before that let's go back to communication that's happening between our brain and ovary.
4. **'Brain to ovary, brain to ovary, release the egg!'** The largest, plumpest egg is the one that will pop out of the ovary and into the Fallopian tube through fine hairs that catch it and carry it down. All the other eggs that started to grow, shrink and fade away into the ovary.

   This whole process (where the eggs grow and one eventually pops out into the Fallopian tube) is called **ovulation** and takes from 11–21 days. The next 14 days is what happens for the rest of your period if that egg doesn't get fertilised. Here is what happens:
5. **The egg is carried into the Fallopian tube.** 'Ahh, yes, we have the egg, and what a cutie it is! The egg is safe and sound and resting, waiting for possible sperm (that's the male sex cell)—hubba hubba!'

   At the end of each of our Fallopian tubes is an opening with little fringe-like tentacles which look a little like sea anemones, which carry the egg into the actual tube. Inside the tube are fine hairs or follicles that catch and sweep the egg further down the tube. Here the egg rests for about 2–3 days. It's waiting because this is where it is likely to meet and be fertilised by a sperm. By the way, the only possibility of that happening is if a man and woman have sex. If that happens and the egg successfully becomes fertilised it moves down into the uterus, attaches itself to that wonderful soft lining that's been prepared and will start to grow into an embryo, a foetus and eventually a baby. That's you and me kiddo, we all went through that wonderful first journey!

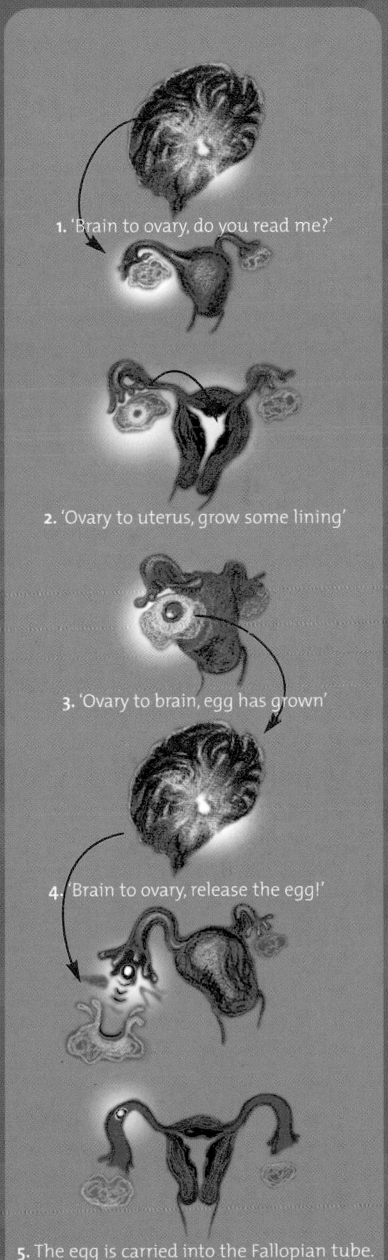
1. 'Brain to ovary, do you read me?'
2. 'Ovary to uterus, grow some lining'
3. 'Ovary to brain, egg has grown'
4. 'Brain to ovary, release the egg!'
5. The egg is carried into the Fallopian tube.

But let's just put the brakes on and rewind here! Zzzzzppp! For you girls out there, what's more important right now is that the unfertilised egg will slowly die away and get absorbed into the uterus.

6. **The last words of the dying egg:** 'Bye, bye, sweet world, gotta love ya and leave ya, nice knowing you, adieu, ciao, see ya later alligator'. Over the next 14 days, when the egg dies away, the lining in the uterus gradually breaks down and starts to pull away. The blood, mucus and tissue that formed this lining start to slowly drip down the cervix and out through the opening of our vagina and . . . Taaa Daaa!—we have our period or menstruation.

The whole menstrual cycle, including ovulation and getting our period, takes between 25 to 35 days. The cycle begins from the first day of one period and lasts until the first day of your next period.

PERIOD QUESTIONS

Dear Puberty Girl
How long will my period last, and how much will there be? I mean, will I like gush or what?

FROM ANXIOUS

Usually your period will last for about 4 to 7 days. Don't worry, this will be a slow leak or dribble, not a big gush. As the lining from the uterus starts to pull away and come out, there may be more blood dripping out the first few days. Towards the last days of your bleeding this will gradually decrease to a few spots on your pad through the day. As to how much blood there will be, let me put you at ease. It's only about a third of a cup. The official figure is about 30–80 mls, and for some girls up to one cup. But before you faint on me, remember, this comes out in a slow dribble over a period of a few days, and that amount isn't all blood. It includes some of the lining formed in the uterus (mucus and tissue). All in all the blood part will be about 2 to 3 tablespoons' worth.

Dear Puberty Girl
If I get my first period and then don't get one for a while, am I still normal?

FROM NOT NORMAL

Yes. Each girl will have a different cycle. It will be hard to keep accurate tabs when you first start your period because to begin with, you may get it for a few days and then you might not get another one for about 6 months. And that's perfectly normal. This is just your body's way of kicking into a cycle that is new and all your hormones are busy getting their messages back and forth. It can take about 2 years after your first period to really get into the swing of a regular cycle.

It's a good idea to keep count on a calendar to give you a clue when to expect your next one. Although it is also normal for some girls never to have regular periods. Check out the calendar and tips and steps on recording your menstrual cycle on the Puberty Girl website www.allenandunwin.com/puberty.asp. Give it a go! It could be useful for when you want to plan ahead for special events like your swimming carnival, a slumber party with friends or a holiday away with the family.

Dear Puberty Girl

How big are our ovaries and how big is an egg? And how many eggs do we have anyway?

FROM WORRIED

We have two glands, or ovaries, on each side of our uterus. Our ovaries are about the size of an almond and contain lots and lots of little eggs. By the time you get your first period you'll have about 350 000. Wowww! Yep, that's a lotta eggs! That's why they are so small, about the size of the tip of a pin. Just as well they aren't the size of a chicken's egg, we'd look a little strange!

Having so many eggs is nature's way of making sure an egg will have a chance of getting fertilised. In our whole menstruating lifetime we'll probably only release between 400–500 eggs, the rest are absorbed by our body before they completely develop. By the time we reach menopause, the end of our periods (at around the ages of 45–55), we no longer have any eggs—that's the way it is, no eggs, no periods.

Dear Puberty Girl

Yuck! What about the boys?! Are they going to go through the same changes and be just as embarrassed as us or what?

FROM IT'S NOT FAIR

Don't worry, the boys have plenty of stuff happening to them around puberty too! Here are some of the things happening to them:

- Boys' testicles grow to about the size of walnuts around puberty.
- They have growing pains and growth spurts like us girls.
- They start to get more facial hair, as well as chest hairs; they grow pubic hair and underarm hairs.
- Their voices break (they get kind of squeaky first before they get deeper).
- They have wet dreams (a sticky fluid called semen comes out of the end of their penis when they're asleep).

And they get just as embarrassed as we do about the changes happening to them.

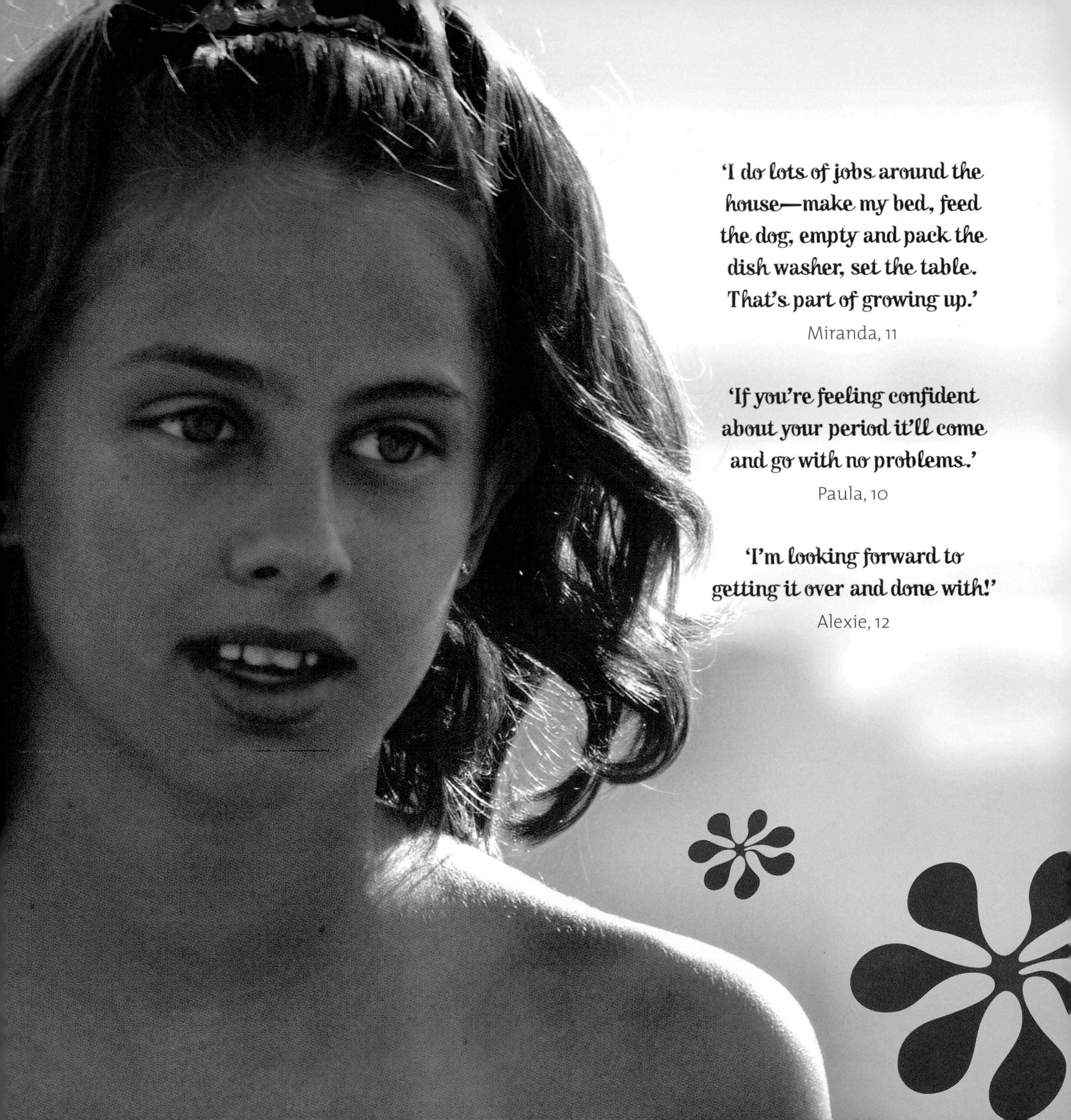

'I do lots of jobs around the house—make my bed, feed the dog, empty and pack the dish washer, set the table. That's part of growing up.'

Miranda, 11

'If you're feeling confident about your period it'll come and go with no problems.'

Paula, 10

'I'm looking forward to getting it over and done with!'

Alexie, 12

Periods and puberty yuck!!! I don't want to change!

Growing up, puberty, changes, feelings, moods, blood—ohhh myyy gawwwd! It can all feel so strange, but after a little while it'll be a normal kind of strange if that makes any sense.

So many girls have discomfort and fear about getting their periods and growing up. It can be a tough time because, on top of all the physical changes, your hormones are causing complex emotional changes as well. One day you might feel great about being wonderfully tall, the next day you might hate the fact that you are taller than most of the boys. One week, you might be happy that you've already got your period and can share tips for dealing with cramps with your girlfriends, the next week (when you have those cramps!) you might wish you could stay a little girl forever!

It is completely normal to have mixed feelings about all that is going on in your body. Talk with your girlfriends, your sister or mother, your teachers or another woman who has already reached adulthood. Every woman you know has been through the same changes and will understand what you're going through! Soon, you might be able to help someone else, too.

I've listed the sort of answers, tips and support that I've shared with girls in my groups. I hope these will help you feel more prepared about some of the changes you may be going through. I've tried to answer the 5 most common complaints I hear from 9- to 12-year-old girls:

Complaint 1: Yuck! I don't want to grow up and change, if it means having more responsibility and I can't be a kid anymore. I like being a child.

Okay, okay I'll be straight with you, growing up does have more responsibility and it's true you're not a kid any more . . . but, at the same time, you still are. Being a kid is something you feel deep inside yourself no matter how old you are. If being a kid means playing games, fooling around and having lots of cuddles, that doesn't have to change. And, besides, the other side of the coin is that growing up means you can get some pretty hot privileges!

For example, being more responsible means your parents trust you to do things like going out to the movies and to parties alone with your friends. You may stay up later, be allowed to cook your favourite recipes, choose the sort of clothes you'd like to wear when you go shopping and choose the sort of friends you want to hang out with. Making more decisions for yourself is a big plus. Oh, and how can I forget. A big part of growing up is starting a relationship and all the smoochy, smoochy stuff that goes with it.

Complaint 2: All that blood—it's messy and gross!

Well as you've probably gathered by now, (if you've read the first two chapters) it really isn't all that blood; it's about a third of a cup, slowly dribbling out over 3 to 7 days. What I usually say to girls about comments on blood and mess is to imagine when they first learned how to go to the toilet without a nappy! Did any of them think, 'Yuck, poo!'? I don't think so! I think you wiped away to your heart's content, because it's your body and you're the boss of it! The only thing that you may feel uncomfortable about is if you get some blood spilt on your underpants while at school. No-one but you should see this and usually it's not enough to worry about until you're home and can take them off to be

washed. The best way to get blood out of your knickers is to wash them straight away or soak them in cold water.

Complaint 3: How embarrassing, I'm going to be getting boobs, and kids at school will tease me, especially the boys!

It's really hard to miss boobs, they're sort of there, no denying it, yep, 1, 2, boobs. You can't really hide them. Even if you slouch a lot, it can just look like you're trying to hide your boobs, which could get you more unwanted attention. It's different with boys since their most private puberty changes are in their private bits, even though they have that embarrassing thing where their voice goes squeaky when they talk. The best thing you could do is to practise telling yourself you are okay just the way you are. Hold your head up and walk proud like you mean it. Ignore any teasers or tell them to stop and walk away. All power to you, since someone who is teasing is generally doing it to get a reaction from you.

But sometimes trying to ignore the teasing doesn't always work. I don't know, I guess some people are just plain thick. Anyway or either way, what we found in our groups is that when ignoring doesn't work it is important to be able to confront the teasing. Attempting to put a stop

to it earlier rather than later will make life a lot easier all around, especially if you've got a supportive friend/s with you. If you're alone at the time then stand tall and proud and be your own best friend in that moment, even if your knees might be shaking a little. The first step is to turn around, look the teaser in the eye and firmly tell them to stop! This might sound a little like Oprah but it actually does work. But! You've got to say it like you mean it! Your facial expression has to match your words and tone of voice.

Here are a few sample responses you might like to try. You might want to practise with a friend or do it in front of the mirror until you feel comfortable with it:

Teaser: 'Hey, look at your boobies, they sure do wobble Harr arr, snort, harr, arr!'

Puberty Girl: (option 1) 'Stop! Making jokes about my body is not okay!'

(option 2) 'If that's your way of trying to make conversation then it's not working for me. Goodbye.'

(option 3) 'Having breasts is a normal, natural part of growing up, you shouldn't laugh too soon, you've got your own changes happening.'

(option 4) 'I'm proud of growing up and maturing. If you've got a problem with that then you need to talk to your parents about it.'

What we found particularly useful in our groups was when the person had the support of their friend next to them and if their friend actually backed them up in what they said. For example, 'Hey, you're being nasty. Having breasts is a natural part of puberty and growing up!' (Check out Chapter 8 for more useful info on working through conflict and dealing with teasers.)

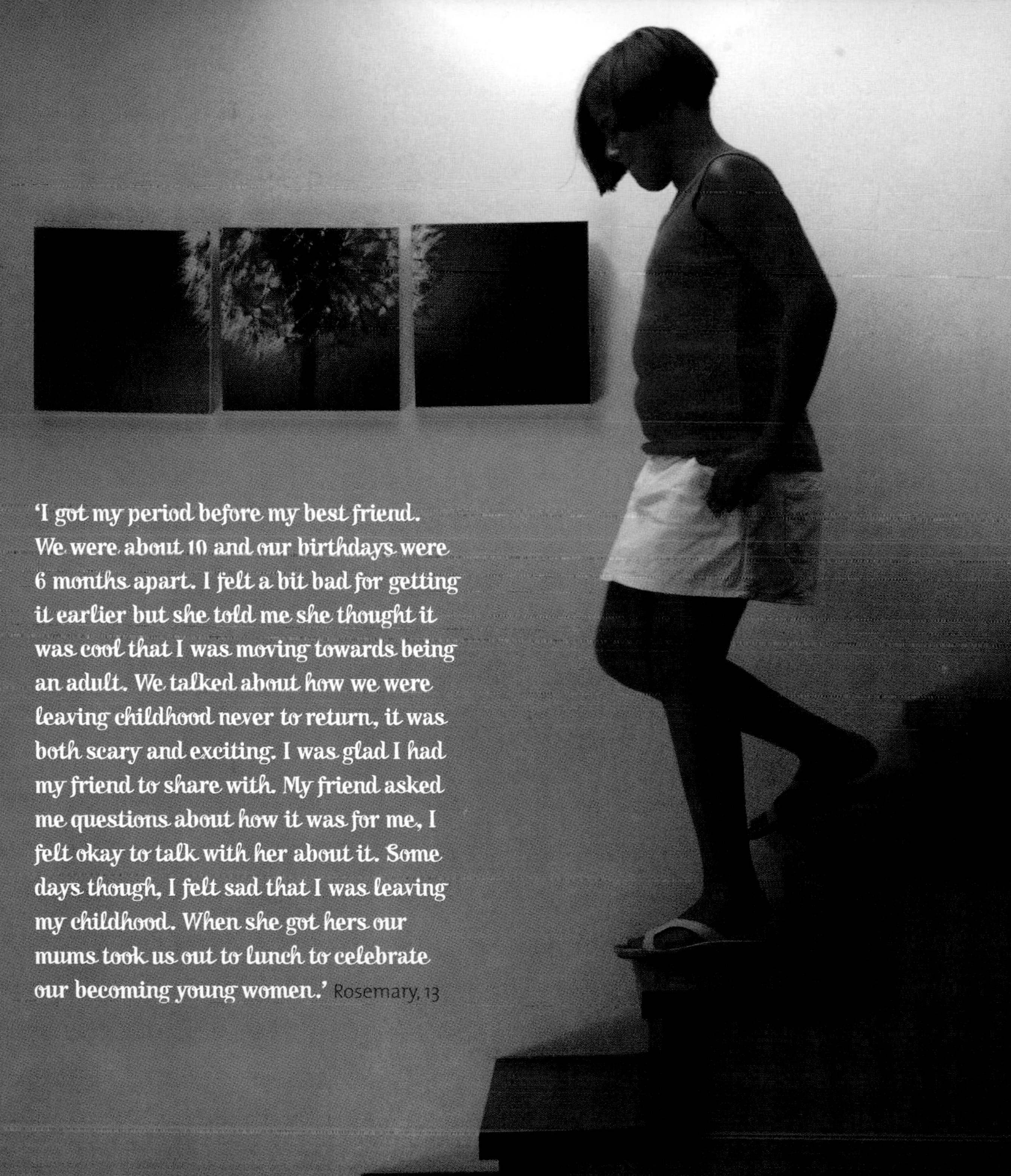

'I got my period before my best friend. We were about 10 and our birthdays were 6 months apart. I felt a bit bad for getting it earlier but she told me she thought it was cool that I was moving towards being an adult. We talked about how we were leaving childhood never to return, it was both scary and exciting. I was glad I had my friend to share with. My friend asked me questions about how it was for me, I felt okay to talk with her about it. Some days though, I felt sad that I was leaving my childhood. When she got hers our mums took us out to lunch to celebrate our becoming young women.' Rosemary, 13

Complaint 4: I'm scared I'm going to be the first one in my class/school to get her periods and then everyone will find out and they'll gossip about me!

It's very hard for anyone to know that you've got your periods unless you tell them. It would be even harder to find out whether you were the only one, considering how many girls would be in your class and your school. You'd have to ask every one and there's a good chance they wouldn't tell you because they want to be just as private about it as you. But let's just say people did find out you had your periods. So what? Isn't every other girl going to get them too if they haven't already? I remember being really worried about being the only girl with pubic hair in my class. I already had boobs and felt really different to other girls who had smaller boobs or no boobs. Then one day after going swimming for sport I noticed in the changing rooms that another girl had pubes too! I was so happy, I nearly did a jig! It made me aware that just because I hadn't been told or hadn't seen the changes in other girls, it didn't mean that they weren't happening.

Complaint 5: I don't want to get PMS and cramps. It sounds painful!

PMS (or PMT) stands for **premenstrual syndrome** (or premenstrual tension). 'Pre' means 'before' so it is a feeling or mood we can feel just before we get our periods. Pimples or greasy skin, sore breasts, headaches, irritability, bloating and feeling tired are all common PMS symptoms. Other 'symptoms' are kind of funny. For instance, a lot of women say that right before their period begins they get a strong urge to clean the house, or organise things, even if they are slobs for the rest of the month. Some women have strange food cravings or eat more than usual. Other women cry very easily before their periods, not because they are sad, but because everything seems to touch their heart.

It can feel like we haven't had enough sleep, where we can feel grumpy, a little moody or fuzzy in the head. We may feel down, want more space and privacy and may be more quiet than usual for no reason in particular. If your PMS symptoms bother you there are many things you can do to make that time better.

Women get bad press about PMS—they make jokes about it on TV shows where the guys nudge each other around a gal who's been teary or angry saying, 'Ooooh watch out! It must be that time of the month', usually followed by eyes rolling and sniggers!

Maybe you've experienced PMS or seen your mum or sister going through these symptoms. It can get pretty messy and generally people might want to duck for cover. My best advice is to let out your steam in small bursts and follow your feelings. How's this for something novel? If you're feeling sad, let yourself feel sad. Isn't that truthfully who you are in that moment? Wooo! Now that's information for free! Even when we think we're reeeeaally good at pushing down our feelings, I think after a while little cracks start to show. It might come out as teasing, jokingly putting someone down, being snappy or gossiping. Again, you might have been on the receiving end of this. Of course you would never do that, would you?

Practical tips for the premenstrual syndrome gal (PMS—sometimes known as Pretty Mad Sister!)

These are a bit like grandma's handy hints for PMS since most of them are based on good old common sense and things girls and women have been doing for themselves for many years. I suggest you use these points as a lifestyle change for general good health, rather than doing a few things just before your period because you are afraid of PMS:

If you're tired –Helloooo, get some sleep! Yes, I know that can be tricky when you're at school, but make sure when you get home that you have an early night's sleep. Avoid having coffee, tea or chocolate and sugar hits because they'll keep you awake and you can crash and burn big time. Those sugar downers can be real downers! You know what I'm talking about girlfriend!

Make 'you' time! If you're feeling crampy, tired and a little grumpy,

you may want to be a little more quiet and hang out alone for a bit. This can be a great opportunity to be creative—writing, drawing or reading are all good things to do when chilling out.

Drink lots of water. We need water to survive. Our body is made up of around 70 per cent water, and our brain and muscles contain as much as 75 per cent water. Water helps to flush the system and keep our body hydrated. It can also help PMS-related fluid retention in our legs and ankles.

Eat plenty of live food! That's fresh fruit and vegies! Don't worry, they won't scream when you chomp into them. Fruit and vegies are rich in vitamins and minerals which is a menstruating girl's best friend! Don't forget those dark green leafy ones. Raw vegies are great snacks; when you cook them, keep it light (steam, stir-fry or dry bake). Fruit is an excellent snack between meals or as a breakfast. Try to include 2–3 pieces of fresh organic fruit daily. Fresh fruit is better than juice because you get all that fibre (you know, the stuff that helps you go to the toilet!).

Go organic. It might be a little more expensive but organic and biodynamically grown meat, eggs, milk, fruit and vegies will be free of pesticides, chemical fertilisers, antibiotics and growth hormones, and they taste better too.

Eat less red meat. Yes you need meat for iron, but a serve of meat should be no larger than the palm of your hand. Choose lean, organic meat and avoid processed meat. Eating less red meat and salt will really help girls who get fluid retention, weight gain, swelling of feet and arms, breast tenderness or tummy bloating.

Get those essential fatty acids. These are found in fish, nuts and seeds. You might have heard about the good oils in some fish. Well you heard right! Mackerel, salmon and tuna have heaps of Omega 3 oils and essential fatty acids that help form 'friendly' prostaglandins that ease cramping. Oooh your body will just lurrrv that!

Make sure you get enough protein, especially if you're vegetarian. If you are not eating animal protein make sure you get a combination of other foods that contain amino acids. These include nuts, whole grains and seeds, pulses and legumes (this includes soy products such as tofu and tempeh). Combine at least two of these groups to form complete protein combinations. Tofu can sometimes create bloating and wind-related cramping so it's best to eat fermented soy products like tempeh, shoyu and miso.

GO THE VEGO— A COMMON QUESTION FOR THE PUBERTY GIRL

Dear Puberty Girl
I'm thinking of becoming a vegetarian but I've heard there are lots of different types of vegetarians. I have no idea which one is the best to choose. Please help.

GRETEL GREEN FROM MT BROCCOLI

Dear Gretel
It is true there are different types of vegetarians or, as I like to fondly call them, 'vegos'. These can range from people who don't eat meat or use any type of animal product to those who eat cheese and eggs. The most important thing is that you're getting iron and all the nutrients and proteins in your diet. This is what usually scares people about going vego. Like, you can't just cut meat from your diet and continue to eat chips, soft drinks and chockies. Being a vego means you've got to plan ahead. You need lots of different vitamins and minerals to make sure your health is good. There is heaps of information on the web that you can check out. To learn more about vegetarianism, log on to **www.vrg.org**, **www.peta.com**, **www.vegfamily.com** and **www.vegsource.com** or ask your local librarian to help you find a good book on being a vego. In the meantime here are the most common 'types' of vegetarians:

Fishy-chook vegetarians: Sometimes people say they're vegetarian but eat chicken or fish occasionally. Weeeeell, strictly speaking they aren't really vegos but they're cutting out the red meat and mostly eating vegies.

Lacto-vegetarians: They don't eat meat, but they do eat dairy products like cheese, milk and yoghurt.

Ovo-vegetarians: They do not eat any type of meat, but do eat eggs.

Ovo-lacto vegetarians: No meat, but they eat both eggs and dairy. This is probably the most common type and is usually the first step toward becoming a vegan.

Vegans: Vegans eat no animal products. Honey and refined sugar are avoided as are silk, leather and fur.

Raw foodists: Eat only raw food and fruitarians eat only fruit, seeds, nuts and fruit-like vegies like tomatoes and cucumbers.

Eat whole grains and whole-grain cereals. Brown rice, millet, corn, quinoa and oats are fantastic. Watch out for wheat though as it can create bloating and stomach cramps in some of us.

Dump the sugar-fizz drinks. You're going to hate me for this but if you can do it, I suggest you dump the soft drinks and especially cola from your diet! Did you know that a glass of cola has 14 teaspoons of sugar in it? It also contains a strange cocktail of caffeine and chemicals. If you want the bubbles try mixing fruit juice with fizzy mineral water or soda water. Make your own refreshing drink with lemons and mineral water. Add a little sugar to taste. It's cheaper and heaps better for you!

Warning, Warning, Warning! The sugar and salty fried food gremlins will be on the prowl around your period. Be a strong Puberty Girl and try to avoid these, especially a week before your period when you are most likely to get PMS! They are going to be the worst things you can do to those hormones flying around in your body. When you get hungry and want to snack, go for foods that release sugars into your blood slowly, to help maintain your energy levels. These are called **low glycaemic index** or low-GI foods. These foods raise blood sugar smoothly and slowly. Chocolate will give you a mega-high hit for a very short time and then drop you like yesterday's garbage, leaving you feeling exhausted, grumpy and down! The low-GI foods are vegetables, fruits (but not bananas), pasta, baked beans, pulses, lentils, bread containing whole grains, porridge, yoghurt and milk.

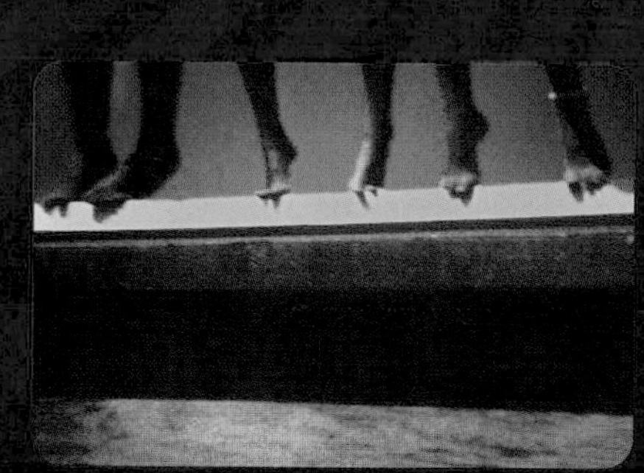

Ouch—I've got cramps!

Part of PMS is that you can get cramps as well as bloating, possible swollen legs and sore breasts. I hope this isn't all sounding like you're going to turn into some swollen up, farting troll with a bad attitude! This stuff is what all of us gals have gone through and thank the blessed cramp fairies that you can do something about managing it. You may get cramping just before your period or as the period comes, but you'll be relieved to know that over the first day or two the cramping eases off.

Period cramps can vary from girl to girl, woman to woman. Some might experience tiny aches and twinges in their lower belly which are hardly noticeable, and for others cramping can feel like something is squeezing your belly really, really hard. Other signs can be:

- strange shooting pains that go down from your hips to the outsides of your thighs
- your lower back might hurt
- you might feel fullness or pressure inside your abdomen that finally eases once you start to bleed

Typically, cramps start 2 to 3 years after your first period. They are most common in women aged 17 to 25. By their late twenties or after giving birth many women stop experiencing these cramps. Some girls don't get any cramps and you might be one of them.

What causes cramping?

When the lining of your uterus sheds during menstruation it has to pass through the cervix so it can leave the body. The uterus contracts (squeezes) to do this, pushing the menstrual fluid out. These contractions are like a mini labour, so in a way you could authentically say to your friends, 'Hey gals! I just gave birth to a period!' Don't wait around for any applause. Prostaglandins are the hormones that can cause blood vessels to narrow, and during our periods they can slow the oxygen going to your uterus through our blood vessels. This can make the contractions in our uterus more painful.

Dear Puberty Girl
Why do my breasts get sore before my period?

FROM LIKE IT OR LUMP IT

Dear LIOLI
Like most parts of the body, breasts can be sore from time to time. Not only for girls, but for guys, too. You may have noticed a slightly sore feeling when you're getting dressed or if someone accidentally bumps into you.

One of the most common times that breasts might feel sore is when they are beginning to develop and especially when we start to form breast buds. We can also get sore breasts around the beginning of our period because a week or so before our period starts our bodies begin producing lots of female hormones, oestrogen and progesterone, which make our bodies retain water, which can make us feel puffy in our hands, ankles and breasts. This fluid can make the breast tissues expand and stretch the nerves, which is why our breasts might start to feel achy or tender.

What can you do about the soreness? It will usually ease off once you start your period. Make sure you're wearing a comfortable supportive bra (avoid underwire bras if they hurt). Follow some of the suggestions I've made for PMS and if you're worried about any pain, always talk it out with mum or dad and maybe even see your family doctor.

Ways of dealing with cramps—painkillers

It's understandable that when we're in pain our immediate response is: 'Eeek! Get rid of this pain and get rid of it now!' Taking painkillers can feel like magic—just a little tablet and all the mean painy wainy goes bye-bye. Painkillers can give fairly immediate and welcome relief especially if you have to go to school, have a concert or exam you can't miss and generally aren't able to duck for cover under the doona with a warm hottie on your tum (which I think is a good alternative if you can wing it).

But I don't think painkillers are the only option for dealing with pain. I see it as part of a lot of options that are lifestyle-based and keep you in control of what goes into your body. Usually when we have pain it's our body's way of telling us to slow down or stop. Ideally, I'd like to tell all my puberty girls to go easy on their bodies and rest up when they have cramps, but I know that's not always possible. Relying only on painkillers over the long term can harm your stomach, liver and digestive tract, so before you gulp down those pills have a little read of my alternative remedies.

Some of the dietary things I've mentioned for PMS will certainly help and I've also included some really easy exercises, home remedies and alternative treatments. Why don't you explore some of these and see which ones work for you?

'I know we'll make it through all the stages of growing up even if we're fragile now.' Katelin, 11

Heat and chill

Have a lie down and have a hot water bottle over your tummy. The combination of heat and weight can work wonders on easing crampy pain. If you've got a cat there's nothing more yummy than having your purring moggy sitting on your tummy! Close your eyes and relax, take in a few slow, deep breaths and let them out slowly through your mouth. If you're doing it right you'll notice your kitty cat rising up and down on your belly. If you find yourself drifting off to sleep, then so be it. Sometimes rushing around and feeling stressed can make the pain worse.

Simple relaxation: Lie flat, preferably upon a rug or mat on a hard surface such as the floor. Let your arms rest by your side, parallel to the body, palms facing upwards. Keep your legs straight, but do not stiffen them. Let your feet flop out to the sides. Relax your muscles and clear your mind if possible. You can work through your body, starting with your toes, alternately clenching and relaxing each part. When you have relaxed your body, breathe deeply and noiselessly from the diaphragm 4 or 5 times. Awaken slowly, turning to your side before sitting up and then standing.

Exercise

This is a great way to ease period pain. You may not feel like it at the time but getting up and doing something simple like having a brisk walk, will help the blood flow through your uterus and ease the cramping. I like walking because it's free and you can pace yourself. Exercise also releases brain chemicals called endorphins, which act like natural painkillers that can help shift your mood if you're feeling a little down or blue. Yoga and tai chi are also great ways to make you feel better and keep you fit. Talk to your mum about where to find a class.

Pressure points and gentle massage

Have you tried this before? Using your fingers or your knuckles, press on these pressure points in your body that will help ease the pain.

- Try massaging the bone just above your bottom and on your outer hips where your legs connect to your pelvis.
- The pressure points for women's menstrual bits are around the ankles. This area corresponds to the ovaries and gently massaging your ankles can greatly ease abdominal pain of all kinds including period pain.
- Three fingers down from the outside of your knees there are also points you can press firmly and hold to ease the pain.
- You could also mix some lavender or clary sage essential oil in a base oil and massage your lower abdomen in slow gentle circles going anti-clockwise. This will feel (and smell) great.

Raspberry leaf tea is fantastic (don't mix this up with raspberry-flavoured tea). It is really great for women and can help with cramping. Look for it in health food stores.

Homeopathy, chiropractic, osteopathy and acupuncture have proved to be really successful in dealing with menstrual problems. A Chinese Medicine practitioner may give you herbal supplements for your specific problem as well as treat you with acupuncture. That's placing very fine needles in specific points in your skin to relieve all sorts of body symptoms. I know women who've had really positive results over time—the treatment might require regular visits over several months. It greatly relieved the headaches I used to get just before my periods.

Put some drops of your favourite essential oils into your bath and let yourself float into watery bliss!

Say what . . . you just got your first period and you don't know how to tell your folks?

So, you've got your first period and you're bursting with questions and you need someone to tell, someone to talk to? Talking to someone you trust is really important. So the first thing to do is to decide who you want to talk to. Just think, if you're the first one in your group of friends who goes through this experience, they might be coming to talk to you about it!

So who do you talk to?

What about Mum? Dad? Auntie Jen? Sarah, your big sis? Best friend Amanda's mum? Your favourite teacher at school? Your school counsellor? Choose someone you're comfortable talking to in your circle of family and friends and TELL THEM ABOUT IT. How do I do that, you ask? Read on.

How do you start talking?

For some girls, asking questions or talking about puberty or periods can feel like cringe material, but for others, it can be cool. Which one are you? Or are you somewhere in between?

If you are feeling a bit nervous, just think that your parent, aunt or friend may be feeling just as embarrassed and nervous as you are. After all it's not something we talk about every day, right? Maybe their parents never talked to them about it and they're not sure where to start.

If you've got the right person, you need to prepare your questions and then find the right time. So how would you let them know you've had your first period?

- Would they just find neatly wrapped up sanitary pads sitting in the bin? (ewww)
- Would they see a blood stain on your underpants in the laundry? (not a good look)

Dear
Mum/Dad/Gran/Auntie/
Uncle (you fill in the name)

Guess what??
As from about 5.00pm today, I'm err, well, umm, bleeding, I mean, not bleeding exactly, I'm menstruating.
Heeeeeellllp!!!!!

Yours truly
Jessie

- Would you tell your big sister who would then tell your parents? (better)
- Would you write them a little note or email?? (See the example in the box to the left.)

Don't stress out, follow these suggestions and may the force be with you!

1. Decide who you think you'd be most comfortable talking to. Are they someone who is open to your questions, honest in their answers and also willing to share about their own stories of growing up? When are they free?
2. Think about what you'd like to say or ask about. If it helps write down a few notes or questions on a piece of paper (besides it might be handy to be holding onto something when you're nervous).
3. Think about when and where you'd like to talk about stuff. Atmosphere is really important. So it may not be best while they're running late for work and your little sister is crying. They may be stressed and not able to be with you. Think casual so that it feels more like a yarn together than an interview. Maybe over an iced chocolate at the coffee shop? At home after dinner? In the morning while you're going for a walk together?
4. Do you want to be alone when you're talking? Make sure you ask for that. If you'd like your big sister or close friend to be with you check this out with them first.
5. It might be good to start with getting to know a little bit about the sort of experiences they had. What about when they went through puberty? For example: What age did they get their first period? How did they feel about their changes around puberty? What did their parents tell them about puberty or menstruation? What sort of stuff was going around in their playground? What did they read about it?

chapter 4

the period COSTUME

You can get a huge variety of 'period apparel', menstrual wear, or whatever you'd like to call it. (Just walk down to your local chemist or supermarket and you'll see what I mean.) The more formal, 'let's-pretend-we-ain't-talking-about-blood' name for pads or tampons is **feminine hygiene products**. Can you imagine asking for that at school?

'Ahh, excuse me, Patricia, I seem to be oozing a little, would you happen to be carrying a feminine hygiene product on your person?'

'Why certainly Harriet, take two why don't you.'

You've got adhesive-backed thick pads, thin pads, ultra-thin pads, minis, maxis, super-absorbents, pantyliners, pads with wings, night pads, day pads, straight pads, pads that curve, cotton pads, cloth pads, even black pads and g-string pads!! Huuuuuuhhppp (just catching my breath!). And that's only the pads! With tampons you've got minis, maxis, supers, regulars, the insert-yourself version, the cardboard-tube applicator version, cottons, organic cottons and many coming in your groovy designer packs with some prints that look like you're going on an African safari! Are you familiar with any of these?

Now if you're totally confused by all the choices, have a chat to your mum or aunt and check out what she wears. After all, she's been there done that for many years now.

Pads, otherwise known as surfboards

Since you'll be getting up close and personal to pads every month, let's find out what they're actually made of. Your average adhesive-backed pad (with or without wings) tends to have a synthetic cover with a non-chlorine bleached wood pulp padding. The pad companies tend to be a little shy in giving out exact info on what's in the pads. But most have a rayon (wood pulp) or cotton padding and are covered with a thin synthetic cover that's highly absorbent. Generally, here's a rundown of the different types of pads you'll find.

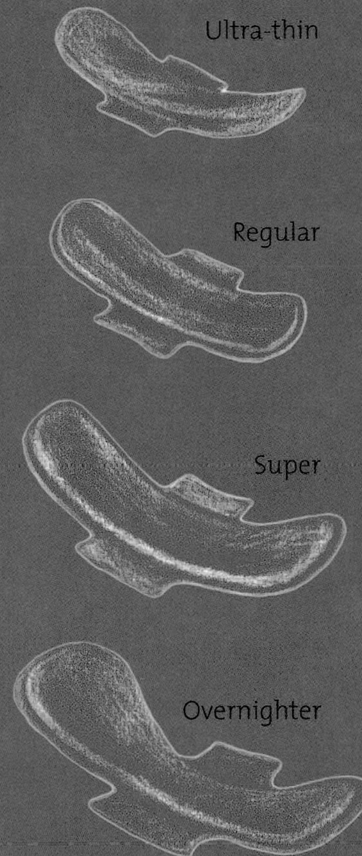

- Ultra-thins: These are super thin but have super absorbency based on the materials used in the pad.
- Regular: Usually for the first or second day of your period or when the flow of blood is lighter.
- Super: When you're in mid-period and the blood flow is heavier. This could be by about day 3 depending on how long your period is. Blood flow can also increase when we are walking or exercising or simply being active.
- Overnighters: Their name lets you know what they're good for. They're thicker and longer so that you won't have to necessarily get up to change them in the middle of the night.
- Pantyliners: These are made to protect undies from mucus, but they can be used when you first get a period if it's extremely light.

All these pads come with or without wings. Why wings? Well this seems to be totally a matter of personal taste. Girls have said that they like pads that have wings because if there is any leakage on the sides, your underwear won't get stained. This is likely to happen when the pad naturally gets a little scrunched up by sitting and walking.

How do I wear a pad?

Golden rule # 1: Before you are about to use a pad or a tampon what do you need to do? Yep, wash your hands with soap. You don't want any bacteria transferred from your hands into your vagina. After you've changed your pad, wrap up the used one in a paper bag or toilet paper and throw it in the bin and then, of course, wash your hands again.

Golden rule # 2: Make sure you place the adhesive part against your undies and not your body. It's easy, just follow the steps to help you along the way. Do this in the bathroom.

1. Wash your hands.
2. Unwrap the pad if it is in a wrapper.

3. Peel back the plastic strip attached to the adhesive backing on the pad or pantyliner. Peel the wings too. Make sure you do this without touching the middle of the pad because that needs to be clean since it's going to make contact with your vagina.
4. It's easier if your underpants are around your knees, with your legs slightly apart. Place the pad or pantyliner on the gusset in the middle of your underpants. If it has wings carefully press them around the outside edge of your underpants as illustrated. Make sure that the pad fits on the gusset of your underpants because if there is any overhang the adhesive bit can stick onto your pubic hairs—ouch, too early for a wax, I think.
5. Taa daa, you've done it. You are now an experienced pad wearer!
6. Pull up your knickers (well, duhh!!).
9. Wash your hands and you're freeeee, to dance, play, sing and have a bleeding good time!

'Even though my mum had told me about periods, I still really dreaded the day that I would get them. Mum had given me a little purse thing with a little pad in it. When I got my period at school, I forgot that the purse with the pad was in my school bag and I ended up using toilet paper until I got home.'
Michelle, 11

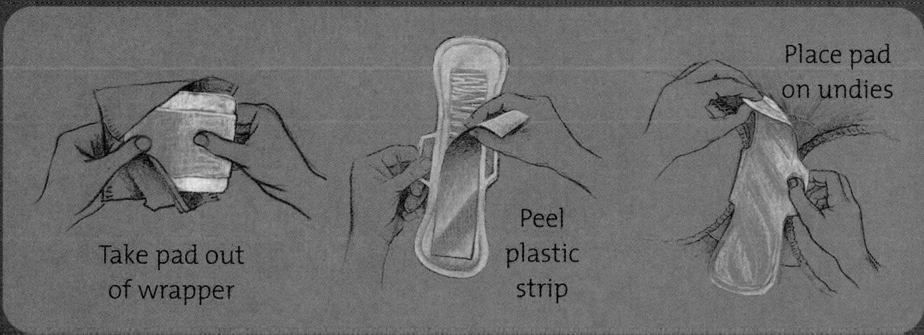
Take pad out of wrapper
Peel plastic strip
Place pad on undies

After a while you won't even notice you've got them on. They may get a little scrunched when you're sitting, walking or crossing your legs. So when you go to the bathroom have a little check that everything is stuck down the right way.

When you first start your periods you may find that pantyliners may be enough. Pretty soon though, you could be working yourself up to a super or even an overnighter! You'll be up there with the big girls saying:

'Yuup! I'm a real bleeder, I'm a super, 4-pad-a-day gal! What do you wear?!' 'Me? Well, I'm working my way up to an overnighter and then ya better watch out, 'cause there ain't no stopping this little bleeder!'

PUBERTY GIRL'S COMMON QUESTIONS ANSWERED ON PADS

How often do I change my pads?

If you decide you're a pad girl, then you'll probably need to change them every 3 to 4 hours. If you're at school, just go to the toilets during your break times and change them or check them. There's usually a sanitary bin in the toilet cubicle. Make sure you wrap the pad in a little toilet paper because the adhesive can stick to the inside of the lid. The person using the bin after you may not like a little paddy-peep surprise when she opens that lid next! If there's no sanitary bin then wrap up your pad and put it in the bin outside.

Will it be noticeable when I walk around in my groovy peel-on jeans?

If you're wearing an ultra-thin pad then you can probably get away with wearing those oh-so-tight stretch jeans. But if you're wearing tights or a leotard for gym or dance class you may notice a little something. Try it out before going out. Check in the mirror to see if the pad's noticeable. Otherwise you may want to consider wearing a tampon.

A message from Mother Earth

Please don't throw your used pads or tampons down the loo. Maybe you've already guessed why. Firstly, because they clog up the plumbing in your home or school toilets. Secondly, and more importantly, they are really bad for our environment. Flushing a pad or tampon down the toilet doesn't just mysteriously make it disappear. One pipe leads to another and they all lead out back to the sea. After stormy weather you may find they wash closer to shore. Truly. Yuck!

◄ Try placing a tampon in a cup of water (as shown) to see how much it swells.

'I tried to use tampons, but I didn't know how. I didn't put them in far enough and they hurt a lot! So I thought that's how tampons were—very hurtful. So I started with pads. Then, as I was getting older I tried a tampon again. I accidentally pushed it further up and I couldn't even feel it! It was like a miracle. I figured out the secret and used them for years and years. In the last year or two I started using pads again because, as it turns out (unbeknownst to any of us for many years), most tampons have toxic chemicals and I don't want that inside of me anymore.

Tonya, 27

Doesn't it smell because of the blood?

Once blood from your vagina hits the pad and combines with oxygen in the air you may get some odour if you leave it for too long between changes. By too long I mean do not leave a pad on all day without changing it. Otherwise you could be losing a few friends. Be a friend to yourself and change your pad regularly.

Tampons—the minties of feminine hygiene wear!

When I was at school our code name for tampons was minties. We might whisper to a friend during recess, 'Hey, psst, have you got any minties, I've run out.' Once during one of my puberty groups a girl asked whether you wore a tampon like a pad in your underpants. Uh-uh, wearing it like that could be preeettty tricky! Unless you've got extra strength elastic on your knickers it will drop out fairly quickly and roll down the aisles looking like an escaped mouse from science class. No, no, no, girlfriends, in case you were wondering, tampons are worn on the inside of your vagina. Knowing how to use them is going to be very useful if you want to go swimming, particularly on heavier bleed days. Once it's inside you, all that is visible on the outside is the little string that fits in your underpants.

The only tricky thing about tampons is getting them in—at first. Once you are able to get your first tampon in it's fairly smooth sailing after that. I didn't start using tampons till I was about 12 even though I got my period at 9. Well, to be honest, I didn't know you could get tampons, then I didn't know how to use them. I found out by reading the instructions on the pack. They were reeeally hard to get in. The trick is to relax. Easier said than done, right? The muscle inside your vagina is strong and stretchy and can tighten if you're tense. So make sure you take in a few breaths to relax first. If you want to try, follow the steps on pages 62–3, but it's okay if you want to start off with pads like I did. For some girls this may not be a choice if they're into water sports, so start experimenting when you get your period, with the help of grownups.

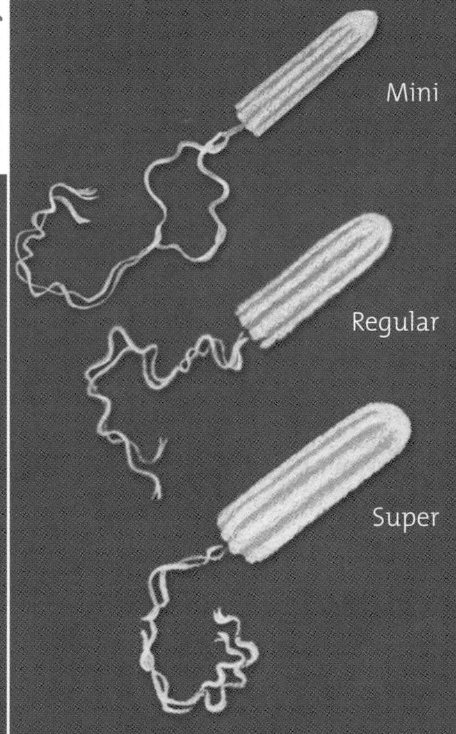

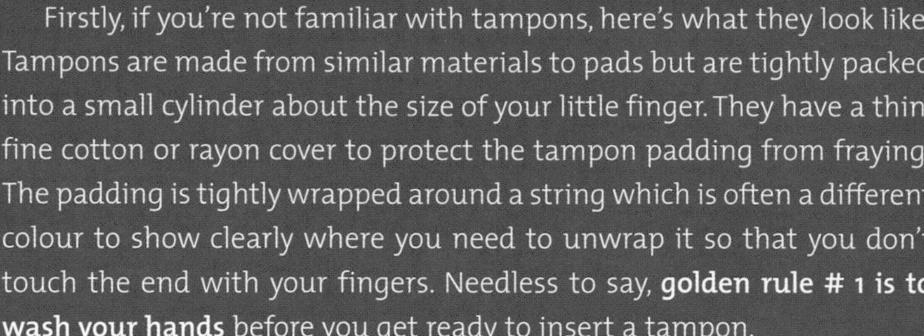

Firstly, if you're not familiar with tampons, here's what they look like. Tampons are made from similar materials to pads but are tightly packed into a small cylinder about the size of your little finger. They have a thin, fine cotton or rayon cover to protect the tampon padding from fraying. The padding is tightly wrapped around a string which is often a different colour to show clearly where you need to unwrap it so that you don't touch the end with your fingers. Needless to say, **golden rule # 1 is to wash your hands** before you get ready to insert a tampon.

Like pads, you can get different levels of absorbency in tampons:

- **Mini** (which are for people like you just starting out) are quite small and have a rounded tip.
- **Regular** are good for when your flow is light or medium, and you can use them when your period is just starting or just finishing.
- **Super** are for heavier flow days and they tend to be thicker and longer and may be used on the second or third day of your period when the blood is dribbling out more regularly. If the tampon sticks or is difficult to pull out after 3 hours then it is too absorbent (too thick) for you and you may want to use one with less absorbency (a thinner one).

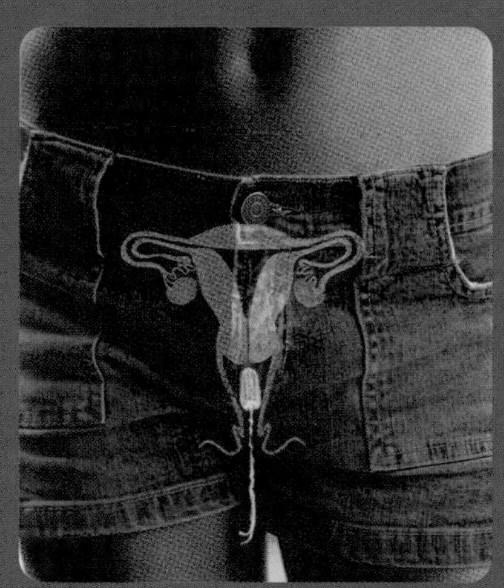

Puberty Girl's sure-and-simple steps for tampon insertion

1. Take a tampon with you into a private room like your bedroom or the bathroom (the bathroom is best because you have a sink where you can wash your hands before and after).
2. Wash your hands using soap then unwrap the tampon.
3. Hold your tampon by its base (you'll see that's where the string is wrapped around), unwrap the plastic cellophane and hold onto the string with your thumb and first two fingers. **NOTE:** If the plastic wrap is torn or somehow open don't use the tampon. Better to be safe with your hygiene.

4. Either squat or put one foot up on the bath tub. With your free hand gently spread open the folds of skin around your vagina called the labia.
5. Take a deep breath in, and as you slowly breathe out, focus on relaxing the muscles around your vagina. While you're doing this slowly insert the end of the tampon into your vagina in the direction of down and back (as if pointing towards your anus). If you push up you'll feel pressure and resistance because you'll be pushing up towards your pubic bone.
6. Slide the tampon all the way in. You'll know it's in right because it'll feel comfortable sitting inside your vagina.
7. Throw the plastic wrap in the bin and wash your hands.
8. Taa daaa, you have now inserted your very first tampon!
9. Make sure you check it after three hours. If it slides out easily when you pull at the string then it was the right absorbency and it's time for a change.

Now having said all this you can also get tampons with applicators. You still have to follow steps 1–5 but instead of inserting the tampon with your finger you'll be inserting the tampon with an applicator.

'I know we'll make it through all the stages
of growing up even if we are fragile now.'
Katelin, 11

Water-based gels—a girl's best friend for tampons

Lubricating gel, also known as K-Y jelly, is water-based and can be bought from the chemist. Get your mum to help you buy it. Put some on the tip of the tampon just before you insert it. If you're a little dry inside your vagina the jelly will help slide the tampon in a little easier. It is water-based so it won't irritate the sensitive skin inside your vagina and it'll wash off your hands easily. Don't use anything that has a cream or oily base, like vaseline cream, hand creams or lotions with perfumes, because you could get an allergic reaction from them and they can interfere with the bacteria in your vagina, and that can lead to infections.

Puberty Girl's 'no question is too curly' answers on tampons

How often should I change them?

You need to change your tampon every 3 hours or maybe more frequently if you are bleeding a little heavier. Your period flow may be a little heavier the first few days and get lighter after that. Because you can't see your tampon, you may forget that it's there! Bad move. If you're at school make sure you go and check when the bell rings at recess or lunch or make a little note.

If you forget your tampon is in, you could run the risk of getting an infection. The worst-case scenario is toxic shock syndrome. I don't want to scare you but I do want to talk about toxic shock so keep reading to find out all about it.

What if I can't get it in? And what if I can't get it out?

Getting it in: If you can't get the tampon in, check to see that you've got a mini. Make sure you're relaxed—take a few deep breaths and start again. Try using a water-based lubricating gel on the end of your tampon to make it easier to insert.

Some girls choose to use a tampon with an applicator. Place the end of the applicator slightly in your vagina, pointing it towards your lower back

First period story

I got my first period when I was 11 and a half. I was at our school swimming carnival and halfway through I went to the bathroom and when I wiped myself I saw brown stuff on the toilet paper and knew right away this was it. It wasn't very heavy so I just went ahead and swam but told my mum about it after the race. When we got home she showed me how to use pads and then she bought me some tampons since I was a swimmer and would need them.

I didn't like the pads, but when I tried to use the tampon it hurt because it was so uncomfortable. My mum got me some lubricating jelly and I think I used that for at least the first year! Melinda, 13

What is toxic shock syndrome (TSS)?

TSS seems to be the only disease with a clear, proven connection to tampon use. It's rare to get it, but the danger is that it can make you very ill and there have been some rare cases where girls have died.

Using any kind of tampon—cotton or rayon of any absorbency—puts girls at greater risk for TSS than using menstrual pads. Sorry to break this news to you girls, especially you swimmers out there. This isn't to scare you from using tampons. It's to make sure you are making informed choices.

The symptoms or signs for TSS can be hard to recognise because they can seem like the flu. If you experience sudden high fever, vomiting, diarrhoea, dizziness, fainting or a rash that looks like a sunburn during your period or a few days after, tell your mum or dad to contact your family doctor right away.

Some things you can do to lower the risk are: choose the lowest absorbency for your flow; change your tampon at least every 3 to 5 hours; alternate pads with tampons and wear pads when you go to bed; know the warning signs of toxic shock syndrome and don't use tampons between periods. And remember to see your doctor if you have any concerns.

Applicator

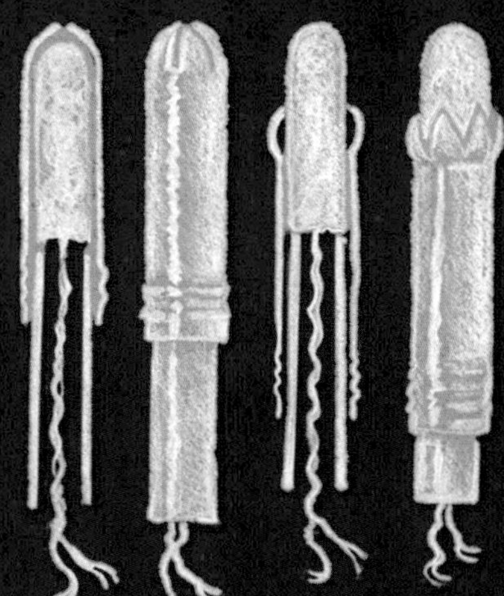

and push it in. The instructions I've included show you how. Some girls have said they found this was an easier way for them. But we're all different and I recommend going with what feels best for you.

If you've tried all the things I've suggested and still can't get your tampon in then STOP. The worst thing you could do is force things. Give yourself a break. It's okay, relax, wear a pad and try again with a fresh tampon later, on another day or even at your next period. Be patient, Rome wasn't built in a day! And your tampons may not be inserted the first time!

Getting it out: Lots of girls are really nervous that if they wear a tampon it will somehow get stuck inside their vagina or that the string will break just as they're trying to pull it out. What I say is that I've never heard of either happening in all my years of bleeding—and believe me that's a lotta years! Have you tried breaking that tampon string with your bare hands??? It's tough I tell you! None of the girls in my groups have managed to yet! But if the tampon and string somehow do both end up inside your vagina they can't go very far. The opening of your cervix is too small and will stop it from going any further. What you'll have to do is use your index or middle finger to try and fish it out. Apart from the icky bit of sticking your finger in, it's fairly easy to get out — remember, it'll be pretty slippery with the blood and mucus etc. from your vagina! If we go with the worst-case scenario that you really, really, really can't get your tampon out no matter how hard you've tried, then talk to a grownup and you may need to see your family doctor to help get it out for you.

Someone said that if I use a tampon I won't still be a virgin

The truth is, a virgin is someone who has never had sexual intercourse. Is inserting a tampon the same thing as having sex? Absolutely not! So where does this question come from? Females who are virgins usually have a **hymen**, a piece of fine skin that stretches partly across the opening of the vagina. Some girls have thicker hymens than others, and sometimes girls are born without a hymen. A female may bleed slightly the first time she has sexual intercourse because the hymen permanently breaks.

It is possible that inserting a tampon will tear the hymen, but that is usually not the case. The hymen usually covers only part of the opening to the vagina. If the hymen covered the entire vagina, a girl wouldn't be able to tell if she was having a period because the menstrual blood wouldn't be able to flow normally outside of the body. In a case like that she'd need to see her family doctor.

Hey dude—like what are the alternatives?

There are heaps of pads and tampons available to you and these include a whole range of alternatives. When you feel up for it, take a look at these: cotton pads and tampons; cotton cloth pads and sea sponges.

Pads versus tampons—good bits and bad bits

Ahh, decisions, decisions, tampons or pads? What are the good points/bad points of using either or both, and which one is best for you? You may want to try a combination that suits you and the sort of activities you're involved in. In the boxes below you'll find the good bits and bad bits of using pads and tampons.

PADS

Good bits

They're secure
You know it's there
They're comfy
You can see them and know when to change them
They're easy to throw away
They're clean
They're easier to use at night
They're easy to pack especially the really thin ones
Using them reduces the risk of TSS

Bad bits

You know it's there
They can give off an odour if not changed
Can't go swimming with them
They can be bulky
They sometimes slip out of place
The adhesive bits can stick to your pubic hair (ouch)

TAMPONS

Good bits

You don't know it's there
They're invisible (except for the string)
They don't smell
They're easy to throw away
They're not messy
You can't really feel them especially when you're first starting your period
They don't take up much space
You can camouflage them in special packs etc.
They're easy to pack

Bad bits

You don't know it's there
Can be hard to remember changing them
Sometimes they leak
Sometimes it can be hard to put them in
Can be uncomfortable if not put in the right angle
Sometimes a tampon isn't enough

Periods yukkkk!!! Pads and tampons are a drag!!! Everyone will tell I've got my periods by just looking at me!!

BY WALKING BLOOD CLOT

Girls in my puberty group often tell me they think walking around with a pad in their undies would be really noticeable. It would be like walking in this gross way with knees bent, legs bowed and bottom sticking out like in an old cowboy movie because of the gi-normous pad that's in your underpants.

Well how about taking a little period test. Which of the following girls do you think has got her periods? If you picked a, b, or c you are correct. Except c is happy because she's a champion rhythmic gymnast!

Getting my periods? It's too messy having to remember to change my pads and tampons

BY FORGETIT

When I get this in my groups one of the first things I ask is: What do you think would have happened if your mother or grandmother or great-great-great-grandmother said the same thing and then magically never got her periods?? . . . This is usually followed by silence then I see a couple of light bulbs popping over girls' heads. That's right YOU wouldn't be here. Little ole, cutesy, tutesy, loveable you!

chapter 5

your body means BUSINESS

Hands up if you have felt some form of criticism or felt unhappy about your body or how you look lately. Did you have your hand up? Hmmm. What did you criticise about your looks? How come? Where did you think you got the message that this part of you wasn't simply beautiful in your own unique way? Let's keep going. Hands up if you felt unhappy or criticised how you looked when you were 5 or 6. Did you have your hand down for this one? Usually there are no hands up or maybe a couple of hands up at this age group. Why do you think there are less or no hands up for when we were 5 or 6?

Well, usually girls in my groups say it's because they were too busy playing and just hanging out and being kids. So where does it all change? Where do we change from hanging out, playing, eating, sleeping and having fun to looking at ourselves and thinking not so nice thoughts? If you think puberty is part of the answer then you're right, but the messages we get about how we look and who we are can start a lot earlier than puberty.

If you had your hand up earlier, you're not alone. Many women, girls, boys, and men suffer from not feeling good about how they look. I'm always surprised to see nearly all the girls in my groups put their hands up for this one. There might be only one or two girls who say they feel cool about how they look and actually like their bodies. I hope through reading this chapter we can understand more about why we do this, and hopefully by the end of the chapter start to practise ways of liking, and even loving how we look and who we are!

What is beauty anyway? We come in so many different shapes and sizes, colours and cultures. I love it that we're not all the same. How boring would that be?

When I sit down with a group of girls and we start talking about beauty, I look around and think wow! You are all beautiful! How come some of you don't think that?? I see so many 9- to 12-year-old girls and they are all diverse in height, skin and hair colour, face shapes, body shapes, eye shapes. I can't honestly say one person is beautiful and

'Beauty is in the eye of the beholder. One person might see someone as beautiful and the other not. I think beauty is maybe love.' Jude, 10

'In the olden days men used to paint fat women because they were considered beautiful then.' Kate, 10

another isn't. To the left are quotes of what some of the girls in my groups said about beauty. See what you think . . .

So, all you beautiful girls out there, let's go on a little journey together, check out the facts from the manure and find out the sort of reasons why we may not feel good about ourselves as we grow up!

'Beauty shines from inside of you. If you're a good person it shines through you and I think that can be beauty.' Samantha, 11

Beauty markers—can you tell me what you think is considered *beautiful*?

I did some investigating on what beauty messages we girls get. Mostly I looked at magazines, billboards and commercials and what we see at the movies and in music videos. I made a list of these and it was amazing to see the similarity of the messages I was getting about beauty. You might want to make your own list before you look at mine and let's compare notes. Here's what I came up with. What do you think, can you relate to any of these?

The messages girls your age are getting about beauty are:

- Buy your clothes from surf shops, Sportsgirl and other designer clothing places to look cool
- Straight hair is better than curly
- Blonde hair is better than brown
- Tall is better than short
- Teeth should always be white, straight and preferably small
- Big boobs are better than small
- Thin is in (except for the big boobs bit)
- Never speak out about feeling good about yourself no matter what size you are or how you look
- Thick lips are better than thin
- Long eyelashes are better than short
- Large eyes are better than small
- Small, straight or upturned noses are better than longer ones that turn down
- Thin, narrow nostrils are better than broad, thick nostrils
- Tanned skin is better than white or black
- A make-up face (especially foundation) is better than a natural face. Although you should wear make-up as if it's your natural face (figure that one out!)
- Accessorise to the max!!!
- Always wear lip gloss

If you have survived these messages and still feel good about yourself, then congratulations—you are one hip chick! You have survived the bombardment of 'LOOKISM!'—that's where your worth is judged upon how you look, not who you are.

Unfortunately some girls do start bombing out and lose a lot of their confidence after reading teen magazines. So much so that they may go to drastic measures to change their bodies on the outside. Fortunately, it doesn't work that way. Research shows that women and teens who are always dieting, exercise long hours or have plastic surgery continue feeling lousy about themselves. I guess that's because they still haven't connected to a beauty that shines from deep within, inside out.

Size does matter

What do you think is the dress size of the average woman?

a) size 10 **b)** size 14 **c)** size 8 **d)** size 6 **e)** size 12 **f)** as big as my Aunt Millie?

If you guessed **b)** size 14 then you guessed right.

70 per cent of Australian women are size 14–16

Okay, so now let's compare this to the dress size of the average model we see in magazines. What do you think her dress size is?

a) size 12 **b)** size 10 **c)** size 6 **d)** size 8 **e)** size 14 **f)** as big as Uncle Frank?

If you guessed size 8–10 then give yourself another tick. Although many models are a size 6–8 which is teeny compared to their height. The minimum height for most models is 168 cm. That's pretty tall for someone wearing a size 8 or 10 so they'd have to be really thin.

If the average woman is a dress size 14 why do you think all these models in magazines and TV commercials are a whole 2 to 3 dress sizes smaller?

The clothing, make-up, facial cream, accessory and shoe companies (that insist beauty means walking around in back-breaking stilts!) all need to make money. And how they make money is to make you believe that how you are naturally isn't okay. That you need to buy all their stuff for you to feel okay and feel like you fit in or belong. For us to feel insecure, unconfident and even depressed is actually good for their businesses because it means you may buy buy buy!! Heard of retail therapy? If you're feeling down, it would be cheaper to talk to a friend or get a hug from mum than to go spending money on stuff that the companies tell you you need, especially when you don't have the mega-bucks.

The truth is that we come in all sorts of amazing shapes and sizes. That's what's gorgeous about us—our diversity. But unfortunately the modelling and fashion industries seem to say that we all have to be one shape and one size: thin. Boo hoo! I say it's time to fight back and fighting back starts with you! Yes You!

Now, you might be thinking, 'Me? But I'm only 10 years old. What has that got to do with me? I'm only just starting to get those breast bud thingies!' Well, that's true—you really are at the beginning of growing up. But guess what, you've probably been getting those messages for a long time. You might even know this stuff already. Usually, girls in my groups can tell me all the famous clothing labels and can name at least one diet they'd seen in a recent magazine. The message we're getting is that how we look is more important than who we are. Let me say straight up—no way! That is not true.

And you know what, we adults cop it heaps as well. A lot of us feel uncomfortable and insecure about how we look, how old we are and what shape we are. We either want bigger boobs or smaller boobs or longer legs or smaller feet or more hips or a six pack.

You might have heard your mum speaking about herself or your aunty, big sister, gran, cousin or maybe even your teacher at school. Any of these sound familiar? 'Gosh, I feel like a pig after eating that', 'Hey, your butt's getting big, isn't it', 'I feel so fat in this', 'Look at her feet, they're as big as boats', 'Isn't (fill in the name) gorgeous, she's so thin', 'Hey, Tracey's lost weight, she looks good, doesn't she?', 'Hmm, isn't that your second serving of dessert (smiling with disapproving look)?'

We all hear and see these messages so much that it can start to roll out of our mouths like a piece of chocolate mud cake with double whipped cream. It's not a surprise then when we join other women in becoming the dreaded infectious 'fat monitoring club'. I've left out the men in this scenario because it seems that the men like us curvy. That's what keeps coming up in those surveys in women's magazines. Generally their vote is for soft, cuddly, curvy bodies that they can hug and hold on to. They are more into size 12 to 14 body shapes than 8 to 10. So why are we so into shrinking ourselves? Because we're constantly bombarded with messages about how we should be looking and we let ourselves become convinced that how we look is about who we are. But it's not! It's only part of who we are—the rest comes from inside, and that's what's most important. Now, I'm not saying grab that cake and eat away to your heart's content—you need to look after your body and be as healthy as you can be. What I am saying is be who you are, not who the magazines tell you to be!

The Incredible Shrinking Woman

Did you know that models 20 or 30 years ago weighed 8 per cent less than the average woman? Now they weigh 23 per cent less.

PUBERTY GIRL'S MESSAGE IS:

Shine from the deepest place within and you will always have rays of sunshine pouring out no matter what the weather is like outside! Your challenge, dear Puberty Girls out there, is to change these old, boring, outdated, limited, yadda yadda yadda messages about beauty and create our own beauty messages! Make friends with other girls who want to change the image of beauty and start valuing yourselves, your power and creativity as girls–women of the future!!

Here are a few suggestions you might like to try:

- Listen to your body. Eat when you're hungry.
- Eat breakfast. It's your kickstart for the day and will help your concentration at school.
- Don't join in, encourage or laugh at jokes that make fun of a person's size or body or looks. Challenge people who make jokes about size and appearance.
- Make a list of the things you like doing as you—not because you have a certain face, colour or body shape!
- Compliment people more often on their ideas, personality and accomplishments than on their body and looks.
- Think of yourself as your own best friend. Remind yourself (daily!) that you're beautiful as you are. Think of yourself as someone who really likes you and wants to hang out with you!
- Be a friend who is caring and treat people with kindness, and hang out with friends who care about you and treat you with kindness.
- Write to the girl magazines stating the sort of differences you want in beauty and bodies, not just the stereotypes of beauty. Ask for models that represent diverse body shapes and sizes and congratulate them when they do it.

Most of all (and this will get tricky) avoid getting into chit-chat and gossip where you and your friends are comparing your body and how you look to other girls' bodies or models in magazines and ads. Do not join the 'fat monitoring club'! If you do start to compare yourself to others, try to remember that we are all naturally different, which means we all have special qualities about us. Make a list of some of your strengths. What do you like to do? What makes you unique? I'm sure your friends could help you in this.

Here's what some Puberty Girls from my groups thought about beauty:

- 'When I see magazines I feel the message is if I want to look beautiful then I have to look like the models in magazines.'
- 'If you don't look like a model you're nothing—you've let yourself down and then you can get eating disorders.'
- 'I think beauty comes from the inside.'
- 'Their eyes (the models') would have dark rings because they stay up late.'

Now let's turn the camera on you for a while. If someone was going to take a picture of you what would your first reaction be?

a) Yeah, cool go ahead, I'm ready with a big cheesy smile or,
b) No way! I hate pictures of me! I need to lose some weight or,
c) Uggh! I look so thin, I need to gain some weight.

If you said b) or c) join the club. On the whole, teenage girls are more unhappy with their bodies than teenage boys. In one survey of high school students, 70 per cent of adolescent girls wanted to be thinner, compared to 34 per cent of boys. Only 7 per cent of girls said they wanted to be larger, compared to 35 per cent of the boys.

With our hormones kicking, it is really natural for girls to gain a little weight especially around their middle. Apart from that we're suddenly getting boobies and hair is growing in places we can't even say out loud. Believe it or not, for some girls, puberty can be like, 'Boobies! Coooowwwl!' But for other girls, it can all start to feel terribly out of control and they just want to scream, 'AAAhhh!, change me back, change me back!'

This is a time when we can feel especially vulnerable and may fall into bad patterns of extreme yo-yo dieting, starving ourselves or pushing ourselves really hard with exercise. Or we might feel so out of control that we start to binge eat—that's like eating, eating and then eating some more. The worst-case scenario is when some girls binge eat and then purge, which means that they make themselves throw up afterwards.

'In the puberty group, I got really stuck trying to say even one little nice thing about myself, when my friend Sandra said she thought I had a good sense of humour and that I had shiny, brown hair. It was a bit embarrassing but also nice to hear.'
Peta, 10

The proper names for these eating disorders are **binge eating**, **anorexia** (girls starving themselves and over-exercising) and **bulimia nervosa** (girls bingeing and then making themselves throw up). You may have heard about these already. I have had girls in my groups put up their hand and say they know someone in their class who they think has bulimia. Maybe you do too.

What actually happens with anorexia?

The proper term is anorexia nervosa and it involves girls (and boys) not wanting to eat because they are really afraid of gaining weight to the point of starving themselves. Even when they starve themselves and lose heaps of weight they still see themselves as fat when they look in the mirror. This is bad for their health and in some really awful cases girls have died. There are all sorts of people and places that can help people who are anorexic. There is an extensive list of references on the Puberty Girl website, so check out the contact details on www.allenandunwin.com/puberty.asp.

Wait! There's hope—what can you do about it?

The first step is to be brave enough to admit to yourself that you have a problem. This might be scary, because you might feel like you're a bad person or that your parents will be disappointed in you. Take a deep breath and talk to your parents for support and go together to your family doctor or counsellor. Even if it is scary for you to admit you have an eating problem your life may depend on it!

'Fitting into a size 8 skirt doesn't mean that suddenly I've got it all together! I think we've all got to look at the whole picture. Growing up for me has also meant sometimes feeling afraid and unsure.
Karen, 13

What's bulimia nervosa?

This is more common than anorexia and also usually begins in adolescence. It has a common cycle of binge eating (eating large amounts in a short span of time and then making yourself vomit it all out). Unfortunately fashion magazines tend to glamourise this by putting in pictures and stories of famous actors and singers who they say have had bulimia. They put in 'Oh-my-god!' type shots in magazines showing them as super thin. I think these can give us mixed messages around thinness and glamour. But believe me there's nothing glamorous about bending over a toilet and vomiting.

Girls who have struggled with bulimia usually say that they started vomiting when they tried dieting to lose weight and they didn't think it worked. The purging or vomiting is usually combined with loads of exercising. I want to be quick to add here that some girls who occasionally force themselves to vomit after eating too much are not considered bulimic and, although the behaviour is unhealthy, studies have found that it doesn't continue after adolescence.

TUM TUM TUM

How to help a girlfriend, Girlfriend!

If you know someone who is anorexic or bulimic, are you worried about how you might talk to her about it? You might want to start by talking to an adult or your own doctor for advice. You can also get in contact with volunteers at the Eating Disorders Support Network, who can provide you with treatment and support options. Check out the EDSN website: www.edsn.asn.au.

Many people who get treatment for anorexia or bulimia are able to do so because of the support from others in their lives. It is often very hard for people with this illness to make a phone call or come in for their appointments. They often need friends and family to take the first steps.

Puberty Girl says, now girlfriend remember . . .

Your friend might ask you to keep it a secret but, girlfriend, this is truly one secret you're going to have to break. I know secrets are important, but the few times I reckon a secret needs to be broken is when it is harmful or dangerous to you or to people you know and love. And this is one of those times! I don't mean going around the playground and blabbing it to everyone who wants to listen. I mean going and speaking to a teacher or an adult about your concerns.

So what is beauty?

Beauty comes in many gorgeous forms: it's rounded hips, freckles, curly hair, straight hair, black hair, blonde hair, softness, straightness, fair skin and dark skin . . . Acchh, the list goes on lassies, and it's times like these that we need . . . Puberty Girl on our side! So, Puberty Girls out there!! What can we do about it???

Have a good look at nature. It's a great teacher of how broad and diverse beauty is. There is nothing more stunningly beautiful than an ageing oak tree or a massive old fig tree, with its big, low, thick, powerful branches. Dolphins and whales don't think 'Oh, my god, look how big my bum is after eating all that fish!' We consider them cute, adorable and loveable just as they are.

chapter 6

Puberty **POWER**

a healthy you!

Oily skin, pimples, zits

Acne is the medical word that covers a variety of skin symptoms like pimples, whiteheads and blackheads. Over the generations of teen-talk, many more creative words have been used to describe acne. Maybe you know some of these like, zits, eye-of-Cyclops, poppers and pus bags. Compared to these, acne sounds pretty tame.

Pimples come from an excess of **sebum** (oil) in our hair and skin pores. And the sebum comes from glands in our skin called **sebaceous glands**. Around puberty, with the extra boost of hormones in your body, these glands tend to work overtime. We all need this oil to help lubricate our skin and hair but pores can clog up with the extra oil and create that red spot on the end of your nose. For most of us the spots clear up by the time we're out of our teens. If your mum or dad had pimples then it won't be a major newsflash that you'll also be getting them because acne tends to run in our families.

As a Puberty Girl you might have started to notice little baby pimples on your face. They appear like little bumps on your nose, just above your eyebrows and around your chin or as enlarged pores on your nose and chin. Go ahead and take a look, surprise yourself—take a quick squiz (er . . . that's squiz not squeeze!). A most common area for girls to get pimples is what they call the t-bar zone (sounds a bit like a t-bone steak!). This is where the pores on your skin are larger and may be more prone to oil blocking them. Mmm, charming!

What's the difference between a whitehead and a blackhead?

The names already tell you the first obvious difference: one is white and one is darker or black. When a pore in your skin gets clogged and closes over it sticks out a little and is reddish with a little white top. There you've got your common household whitehead.

When a pore clogs up but stays open, the top of it might darken and that's what you call your blackhead.

What did one pimple say to the other? Gee I'd like to give you a squeeze!

Pimples can be small and relatively painless bumps that only take a day or two to go away or they can be large, red and painful. Pimples most often appear on our faces, but we can also get them on our backs, necks, chest, shoulders and even our bottoms!

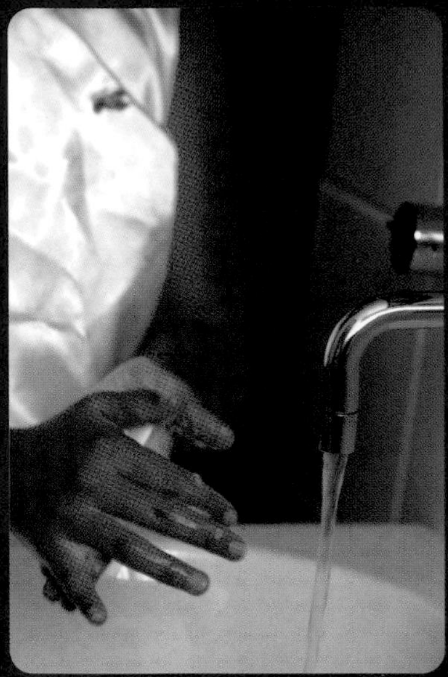

Okay, so I'm doomed to pus—what do I do about it?

You can certainly manage and even clear up your pimples by taking care of your skin. Try and cut down on the oil that's building up in your hair and face by washing more regularly. I remember that before I got my periods I could get away with washing my hair just once a week. Hoo boy did that change! PP (post period) I had to wash my hair nearly every day to keep it clean.

Wash your face twice a day with a mild soap-free cleanser and warm water. You actually don't need a lot of fancy foaming treatments. Of course it makes sense to maybe wash again after exercise if you've been sweating a lot. Be gentle: you might think that scrubbing hard will get rid of the pimples but it might create an irritation which will dry the skin surface, stimulating the oil glands in your skin and creating more oil and hey presto, more pimples!

Try not to touch your face with your hands. Any dirt or bacteria from your hands can be transferred to your face and create infection. Yup, even resting your face or chin on your hands while you're reading this can do it! Wash your hands regularly. I don't mean every 5 minutes but at times like when you've gone to the toilet, eaten greasy food or cleaned your room.

If you use hair gel or other products like that then try to keep it away from your face, as they can also clog pores.

Warning . . . pimple alert . . . warning

Don't pick at, squeeze or scratch your pimples. I know it will be very tempting, seeing that whitehead on the end of your chin, staring you in the face, begging to have its little insides squeezed out. But this can make your

MYTH: Have you heard that chocolates and fried foods will cause pimples? There has been a belief that if you avoid them it'll help stop or reduce pimples. Although there's no medical evidence to prove this you might want to apply some of the advice that grandma gives about eating her chicken soup when you're sick. It might not help but it couldn't hurt! Certainly touching your face with grimy hands after you've eaten a greasy hamburger or a sticky chocolate bar won't be good for your skin as it risks getting bacteria into those pores.

skin worse and may cause scars or tiny pockmarks. Excessive squeezing can also re-stimulate oil glands and potentially create more pimples.

If you really must squeeze what I call a ripe pimple (you'll know what I mean when you see one! It's almost screaming at you, squeeze me, SQUEEEEZE MEEEE!), then I suggest you do the following: Wrap both your index fingers with tissue paper and do it very gently and slowly to pop the top off. Then rinse your skin with warm water and use a cotton ball to dab on some non-alcohol based toner like witchhazel. Witchhazel is a natural plant that helps clean and tighten pores, it's fairly inexpensive and can be bought at your local supermarket. Another really good option is putting a little drop of tea-tree or lavender oil directly on your pimple. These are fabulous natural antiseptics. Hopefully you'll wake up in the morning and bye-bye pimple or you'll at least see some serious shrinkage!

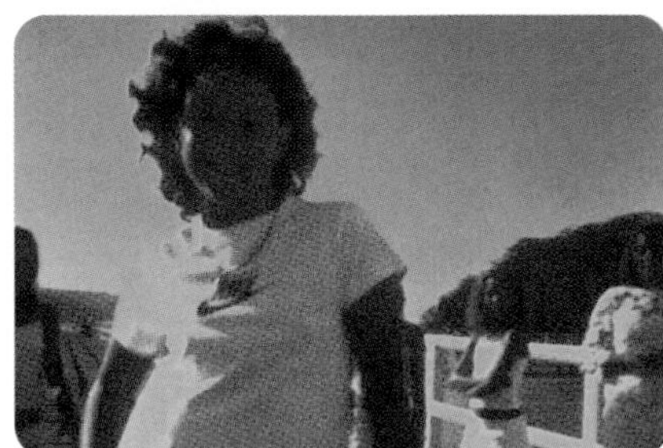

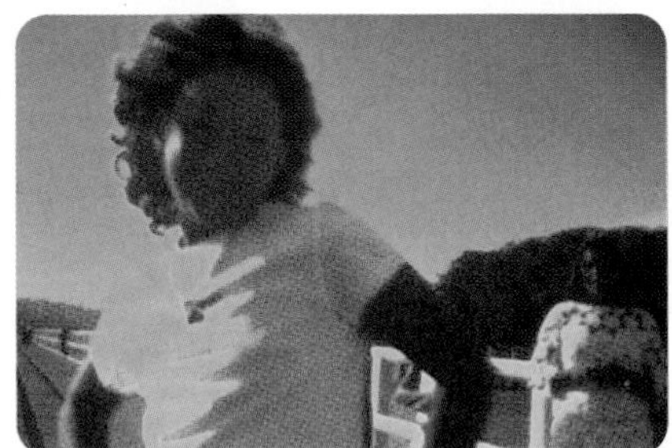

Here a hair, there a hair, everywhere a hair, hair

You've probably noticed more than a few of those alfalfa sprouts growing under your arms and in your pubic region and that the hair on your legs and arms may have darkened. Hair is such a personal thing and I'm astounded at where we can sprout the stuff. Forget pubic hair, underarm hair and leg hair. We can get hair growing under our chins, upper lips, toes, backs, breasts (around the areola) and even our bottoms! In some cultures hairy underarms and legs can be considered sexy and the attitude is more, 'Ooh yeah baby, bring it on!'

Let it be, let it be

Now all you can do at this stage is just sit back, relax and let the hair grow! It's cheap, it's easy, it's pain-free and probably not very noticeable as a preteen. Later on, you might want to consider hair removal but it will cost you money on a regular basis. Talk to your mum or an aunt about your choices.

Body odour—the body's eau de parfum

We all have to sweat. If we didn't we'd probably go into spontaneous combustion since it's our bod's way of cooling down! Doggies cool down by panting. I've tried that, it doesn't work. We do it through our skin. Our oil glands and sweat glands also let our skin breathe and get rid of waste products. Teen sweat is different from kid sweat. For starters, there's more of it. It's like the sweat-o-meter in our body is clicked onto high! The areas that are most affected are our armpits and genitals. That's because one of our sweat glands, called **apocrine,** is found mostly in these areas! Sweeet! Or is that Sweaaaat?? The apocrine glands try and regulate or control the amount of sweat coming out of us whereas our other sweat glands, called **eccrine** glands, let off the salty liquid that's good for cooling us down.

What sets these sweat glands pumping? It's not just a stinky hot day in the sun that does it. We can sweat after we've exercised or when we're nervous, stressed out or afraid.

As long as we've washed regularly, our natural body smells are mostly great. In fact it can be what attracts us to each other. Ever met someone you've liked because they smell naturally good? The B.O. (body odour) factor comes in when the sweat hits the air and doesn't have time to evaporate. When bacteria that is released from the sweat glands under our arms, feet and genital area breaks down, it can leave an unmistakeable musky smell. Yup—that's the stuff that can sometimes take our breath away and not in a good way!

How to keep fresh while you keep your cool

We all have body odour at some point or another and there are lots of things we can do about it. The most obvious is to take care of your personal hygiene:

- Take daily showers and baths. Make sure you use a mild soap and warm water under your arms and around your bottom and genitals.
- Change into clean clothes, underwear and socks every day. Smell those used t-shirts and socks before you put them on; that might be enough to turn you off wearing them again. Don't kid yourself even if you've only worn them once!
- Wear clothes made of natural or 'breathable' fabrics (like 100 per cent cotton or linen/cotton blends). This will help keep you feeling drier because they allow the air to circulate, and absorb the moisture. Avoid clothes made of nylon and synthetic fabrics that don't breathe and trap the moisture.

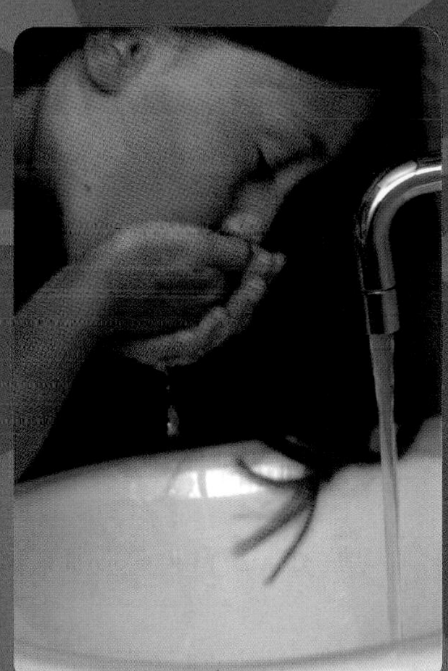

Some people stop here. As long as you bathe regularly and wear clean clothes, the smells that mama nature gave you might be sweet enough but:

- If you drink a lot of cola (i.e. stuff that's got caffeine in it) then cut down because they'll make your apocrine sweat glands work harder.
- And drink lots of water. This keeps eccrine glands active and can dilute the smell from your body. Eat lots of fruit and vegies. What you eat can end up coming out through your pores and will affect how you smell.

Spray it, slick it on, rub it, roll it— deodorants and anti-perspirants or B.O. blasters

The difference between deodorants and anti-perspirants is that deodorants tend to work by covering up the smell but they don't prevent sweating. Anti-perspirants can contain aluminium which actually

Dear Puberty Girl

My friend has what I would call unfortunate body odour. Sometimes kids in the playground make comments or faces behind her back which I feel bad about. Should I tell her about it or let her find out another way?

FROM
ELIZA DOOGOOD

Dear Eliza

Yes, absolutely, tell your friend in a kind way. She may not be aware of how strong it is. Better she hears from you than from someone else who might tease or be mean. Make sure she knows you're telling her because you care about her. Lavender oil is a wonderful natural deodorant!

reduces or stops the natural process of sweating. In the long term this can be harmful since it can create a build up of toxins needing to be released from your body. Anti-perspirants are also more likely to create skin irritations than deodorants.

Tanned and terrific (I don't think so!)

Getting 10 minutes of sunlight everyday on our arms and legs gives us our daily boost of Vitamin D. To stay under the sun for hours during peak times (that's 10 a.m. to 3 p.m.) is literally cooking yourself and potentially damaging your skin. For starters you can get premature wrinkles and the worst-case scenario is getting skin cancers. (Oh, and by the way, getting a tan doesn't clear up acne. I repeat does not. While a suntan may make pimples less visible temporarily, the sun damage to your skin will be a lot worse than having zits by a long shot.)

How tanning affects your skin

A tan is visible proof that your skin is being damaged. When the sun's ultraviolet rays hit your skin, it stirs to action cells known as **melanocytes**, which make a brown pigment called **melanin**. This melanin can act as a natural protection to your skin. The less melanin we have, the less protected we are. For example, if you have an English, Irish, Scottish or northern European background then you'll have less melanin and your skin may be whiter and more likely to burn quickly under the sun. If your background is Indian, African, Indonesian or Australian Aboriginal you may have black or dark brown skin which means it has more melanin and more natural protection against the harmful rays of the sun.

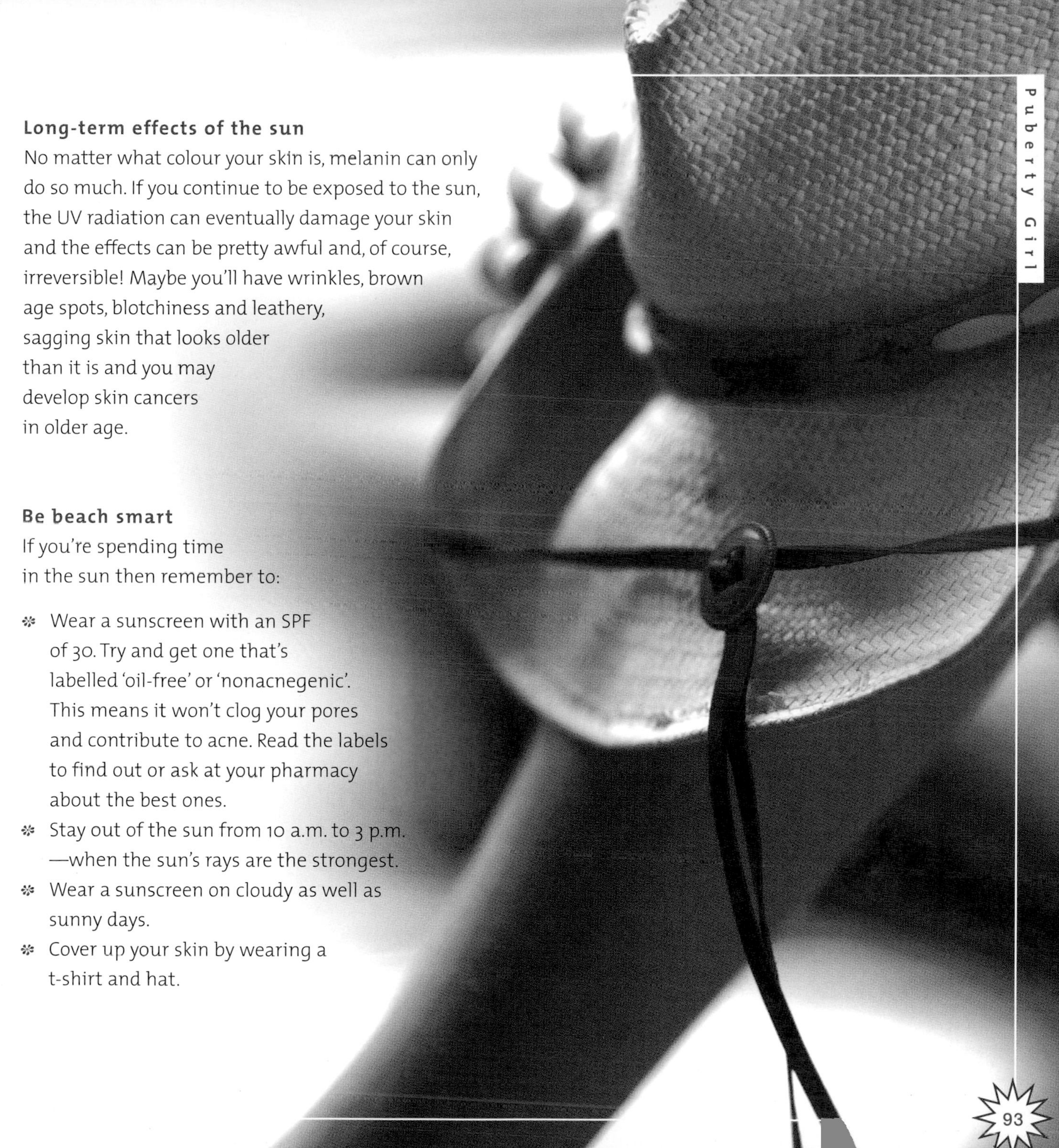

Long-term effects of the sun

No matter what colour your skin is, melanin can only do so much. If you continue to be exposed to the sun, the UV radiation can eventually damage your skin and the effects can be pretty awful and, of course, irreversible! Maybe you'll have wrinkles, brown age spots, blotchiness and leathery, sagging skin that looks older than it is and you may develop skin cancers in older age.

Be beach smart

If you're spending time in the sun then remember to:

- Wear a sunscreen with an SPF of 30. Try and get one that's labelled 'oil-free' or 'nonacnegenic'. This means it won't clog your pores and contribute to acne. Read the labels to find out or ask at your pharmacy about the best ones.
- Stay out of the sun from 10 a.m. to 3 p.m. —when the sun's rays are the strongest.
- Wear a sunscreen on cloudy as well as sunny days.
- Cover up your skin by wearing a t-shirt and hat.

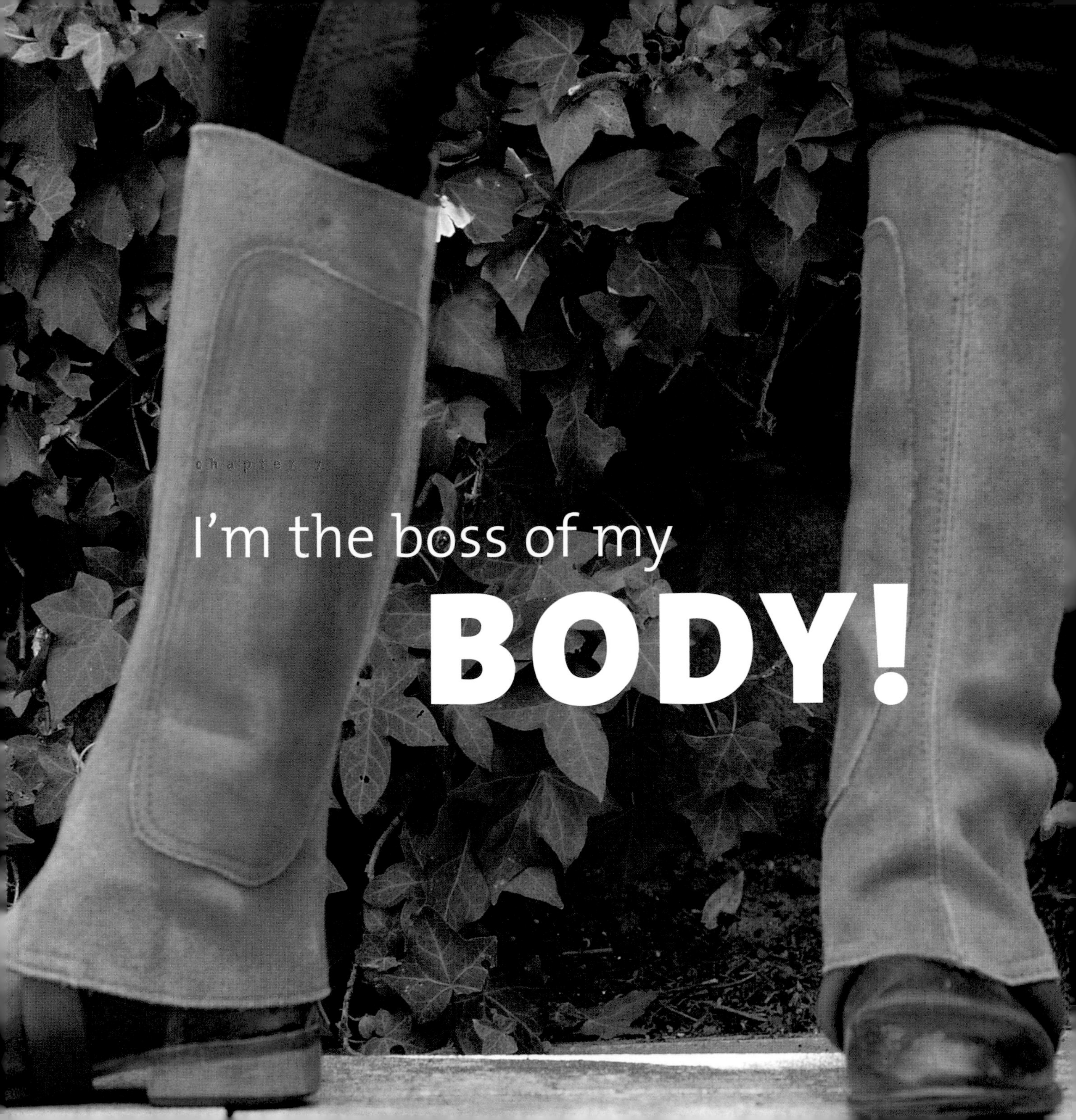

chapter 7

I’m the boss of my BODY!

What do I mean when I say boss of your body? Well, it's about trusting yourself and your feelings. It's being aware of what feels good and comfortable and safe for you in your daily world where people will touch you in different ways. And, importantly, it's also about being able to speak out when things don't feel good for you. To say 'No! I don't like that' and 'Stop!' is part of being the boss of your body.

Most of us have had some information at school about stranger danger. We've been told to report strange men who hang around parks, bushes and children's playgrounds. And we've learnt ways to avoid these people. If they try and hassle us, we know we can say 'No!' to them and run away to tell parents or other adults.

Uh-oh! What about touch that's with people I know?

It might seem like a strange thing to be talking about—touching from people we know because we don't expect to think about what feels cool and what feels ick! Take a moment to think about it now. Who do you feel comfortable with touching you? What sort of touch feels safe and okay? What sort of touch is definitely not okay for you, like makes you feel 'shrinking inside' uncomfortable?

The people we know that touch us can include mum, dad, aunties, uncles, grandmas, grandpas, brothers, sisters, teachers, family friends, best friends. Here are some ways they might touch us: cuddles, hugs, holding hands, patting on the head, scratching the back, squeezing your foot. The list can go on.

Can you name the sort of touch that would not be okay? Where even the thought of it makes you feel sick, uncomfortable or scared? This might include being asked (or pushed) to do things you don't like, maybe touching or patting bottoms, sloppy kisses on the mouth, bone crushing hugs, pinching or rubbing you or sticking fingers in places that are private. Even the very first time it happens can make you want to shout 'STOP IT!

THIS IS MY BODY!' and run away and tell someone immediately! What you need to know is that **you don't have to let anyone touch you in any way that feels unsafe or sexual**. This is known as abuse because it's wrong. Just because we know the person doesn't mean they can touch us in a yucky way. It's also not okay for someone to ask you to touch any part of them that you're not comfortable with. Sometimes this confuses us because they might be someone in our family or a family friend that we're meant to trust or feel safe with. That's why it's doubley, tripley, quadrupley important that you trust your own feelings. If you're getting an icky, squirmy, uh-oh, embarrassing feeling even reading this, I'm pleased. You're alive and tuned in! That's your feelings talking to you!

Keep Unwanted Touching a Secret? NO WAY JOSE!

Don't let anyone tell you it has to be kept a secret. They can be tricksy and try to confuse your feelings by saying things like, 'It's because I love you' or 'It's only a game' or 'If you do it I'll buy you a treat'. Of course, that's a load of manure! These are all traps to make you do what they want you to and to squash down your own feelings. **Remember that you've done nothing wrong and telling someone is the first step to putting a stop to any unwanted touching**.

What can you do or say in those moments??

Finding the right words in these moments is hard because we can feel caught by surprise and a little scared. It might feel so strange that we could start to think we're imagining it. Trust yourself and trust your feelings, Puberty Girl! You have the right to feel safe.

Here are some ways that girls I know have coped:

- **Speak up and speak out**. If there's another adult in the next room, call out loudly for them to come and help. Or tell a parent or adult you trust as soon as possible.
- **Push away**. Try and get away from being in the same room.
- Say 'No' like you mean it. Some other things you can say loudly are: I don't like this! Stop!, Don't do that!, Don't touch me!, My body belongs to me!, Stop it! I'm going to tell my . . . (mother, teachers, aunty, friend).
- **Tell someone you trust**. People you might speak to could be another relative, your friend's parent, a teacher, counsellor, the school nurse or principal. You might tell your coach, minister or rabbi. Pick someone you feel safe with. Keep on telling grownups until they listen to you and believe you and they help to stop it happening again.
- **If a week goes by and no-one does anything to help, tell another adult**. Keep telling until you get help. If you can't get an adult you know to help, there are telephone hotlines you can call for help, any time of any day. A really big one is **Kids Helpline**. This is their number and it's a free call: **1800 551 800**. The person you speak to is someone who's experienced in helping other kids with this sort of thing. You can decide whether you want to talk with a man or a woman.

Who is in your safety network?

Your safety network is people you feel comfortable with. People who you know, trust and of course feel safe with to talk about stuff or ask for help.

Here's an example of a safety network that has worked out for girls: teacher, mum, Dr Tanya, Tod, Peachy the cat, cousin, Aunty Pat, best friend Melissa, best friend's mum.

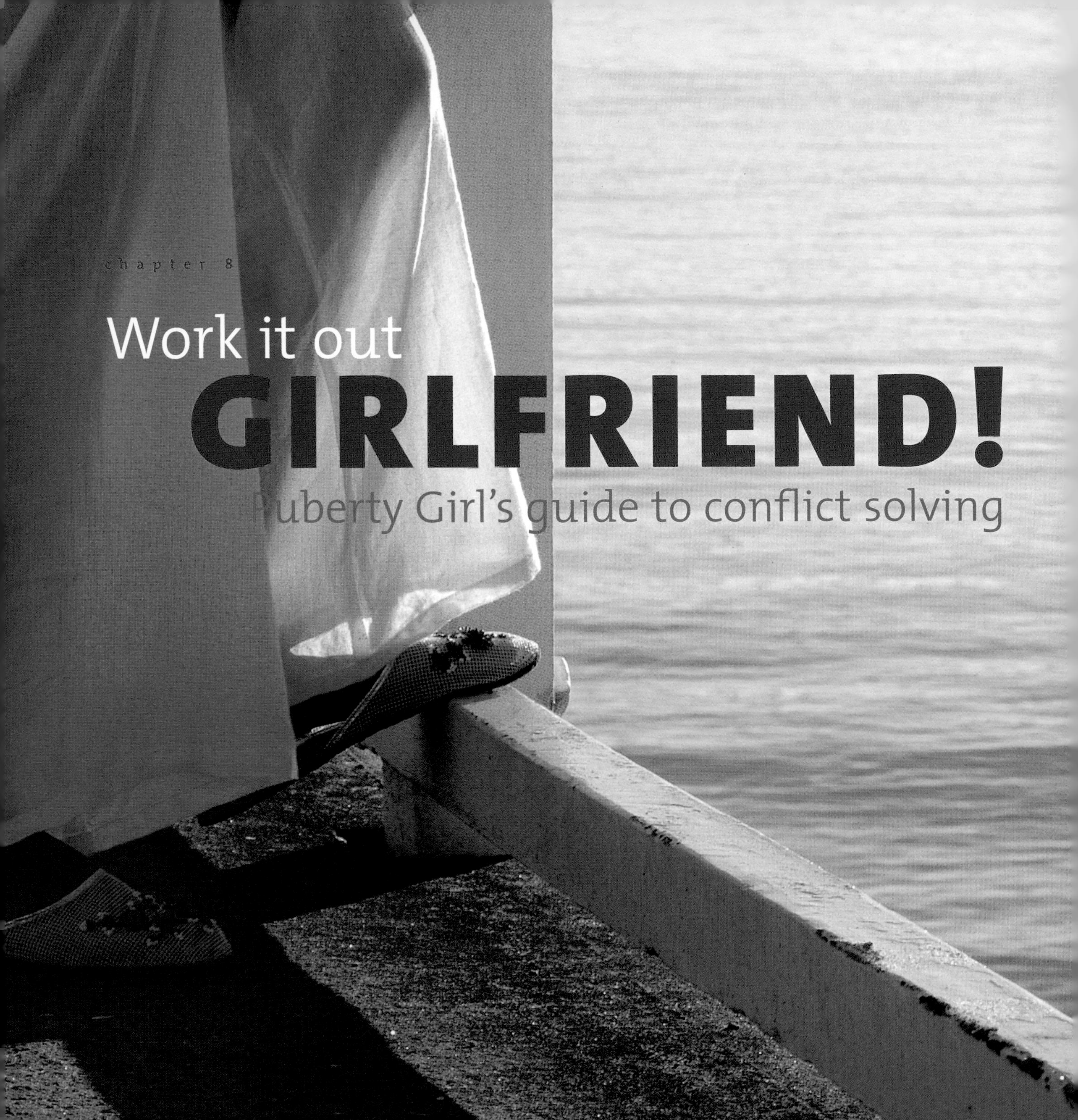

chapter 8

Work it out GIRLFRIEND!

Puberty Girl's guide to conflict solving

I remember early in Year 7 I had a fight with a friend who was really popular and arguing with her meant I was also out of our group—even though no-one had actually said this. I had imagined all this terrible stuff about her, that she was mean and didn't value our friendship etc etc. This went on until the second term when we finally made contact again and I found out she was also feeling bad, was wanting to make contact but felt too hurt or shy to talk to me.

Has this ever happened to you? Have you noticed lately that more and more you're having a misunderstanding with a friend or you're clashing with some friend's personality and that's causing a conflict? Even worse, have you had a problem with someone and left it for weeks, neither of you talking to each other and causing each other problems, like I did?

Girlfriends, the moral of the story is: don't wait! Sorting things out as they come up is the best way to deal with and avoid problems or conflicts. Get those conflict-resolving muscles working. When we can sort out problems, we can understand, respect and love our family and friends even more than we did in the first place! I know it can be scary so here are lots of really juicy tips on how to get into it and get out of it! But first, let's find out what we mean by conflict and the kinds of conflict we might experience.

Conflict—what's it all about?

Why do people disagree or fight? Well, basically it's about difference. We're all different and how we communicate and how we understand stuff is also different. This can be anything from what our family's values and beliefs are, what culture we come from, whether we are spiritual or religious, how old we are, whether we're girls or guys, who we choose to be friends with, our health, whether we have a physical or mental disability, our family's financial situation, and that's only a few. Our differences make up the rich world that we live in but they can also create conflict and tension. The most important thing to remember about our differences is that being different doesn't mean that one is better than the other, so we all have the right to be treated equally and with respect. And that means by other kids as well as adults.

What do you look like when you're eye to eye with a conflict?

WHEN CONFLICT HAPPENS, DO YOU:

a) Jump in, licking your lips and rolling up your sleeves?
b) Try and ignore it and hope it goes away?
c) Run for the hills?
d) All of the above at different times.

If you chose d) then you're on the right track. At different times and in different conflicts we might do any one of these things. Conflict tends to get complicated if we only stick to one thing. For example, running away could be a good option (it's one way of keeping fit!). But, if you find the same conflict keeps happening then you may need to face the music and work on it. Knowing what sort of conflict patterns we have might be a good starting point. Read on and see if any of these might be a little like your friend, your sister, your next-door neighbour, cousin or maybe even you! Remember, it takes at least two people to have a fight so you need to be aware of your role in stuff too!

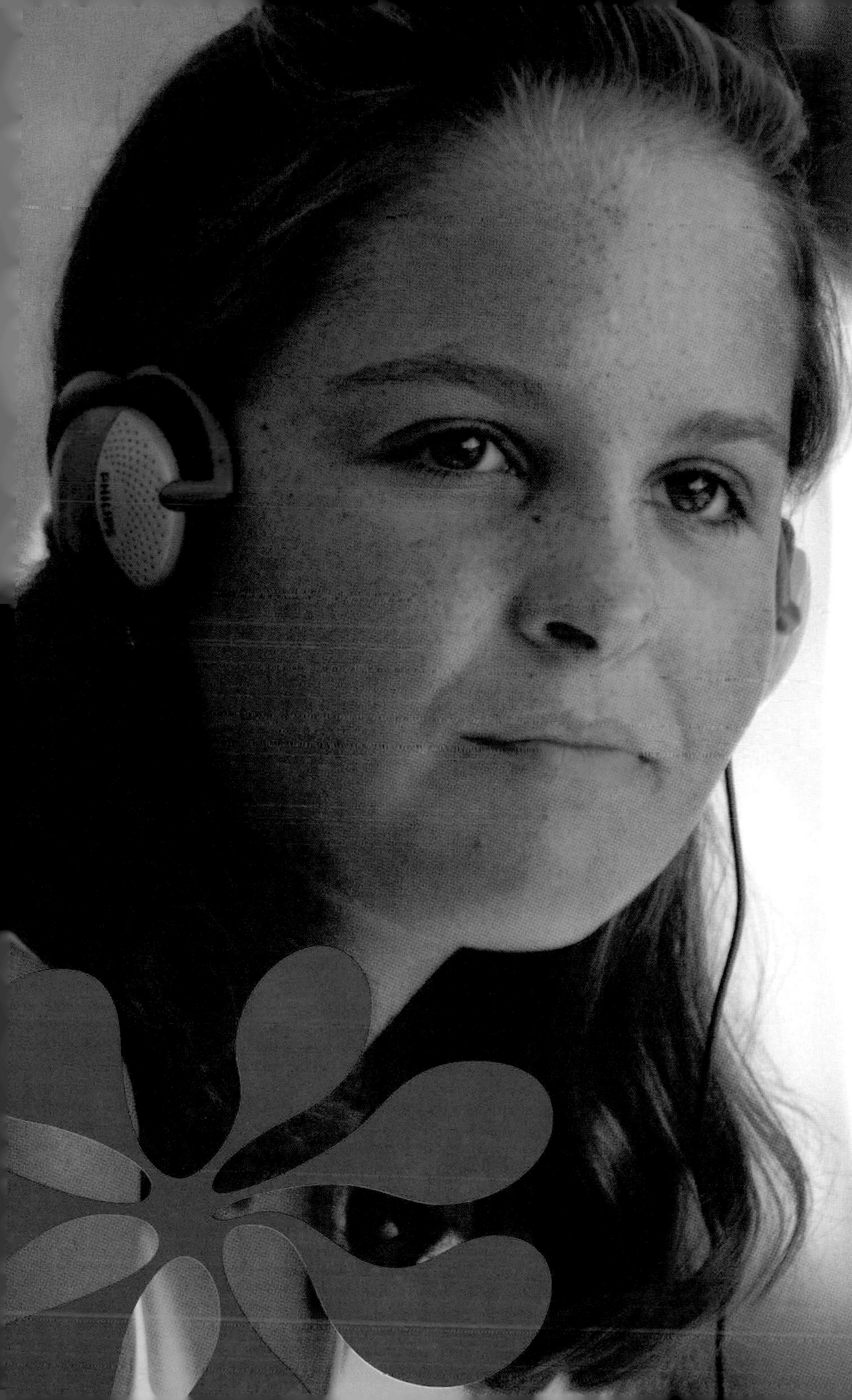

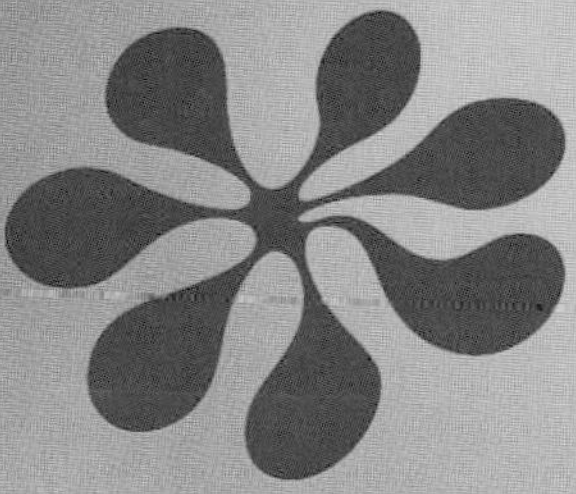

Remember . . .

It's not okay for someone to try and make you feel bad, embarrassed or uncomfortable about your body or who you are. If someone is teasing you for having breasts, pimples or even for getting your periods, then you need to try and resolve the problem. If you're the one doing the teasing, then STOP! Remember that it hurts people to tease and you never know, you might be the one being teased next time!

One thing that definitely does not work to stop teasing, though, is teasing back. Name calling, put downs, smarty pants, sarcastic, nyaah, nyaah, nyaah comments can make you look as ugly as the person who started the teasing. Like sarcasm, it can be really hurtful and it can damage trust and respect with family and friends.

Also, continual verbal battles can progress very quickly into physical ones and, girlfriend, you do not want to go there!

Some conflict types

THE IF-LOOKS-COULD-KILL TYPE

When someone rubs her the wrong way or she's just in a mood, she suddenly shoots sharp, dagger-like shards of ice out of her eyes directly into the heart of her victim, all while smiling! You know the type.

What to do?

- It's very tempting to run for the hills with this one! Try to ignore the bad behaviour and leave them to themselves. You know what? Their bad mood might have nothing to do with you at all. It's best to hang out with someone else or go somewhere else.
- Use humour: Try something like, 'Ouch, I felt a sharp zap just then. It seemed to come directly from your eyes!'
- Be direct and assertive: 'You've now made a couple of sharp comments that have been hurtful. Do you want to talk about that?' If they say yes, great, it could be a chance for you to understand each other better. If they say no, then it might be a good time to say 'That's fine, I'll see you later'.

THE YELLER

(Man, don't they ever get a sore throat?) This one tends to give you a blast of anger and then be over it in minutes, meanwhile you're still clutching your chest in shock! This sort of behaviour is usually saved for a brother or sister, mum or dad and can be about anything from eating the last Tim Tam to something more serious like teasing.

What to do?

- Yelling back is pointless so try to cool things down by lowering your voice and keeping calm. Talk about what's really making them so unhappy.

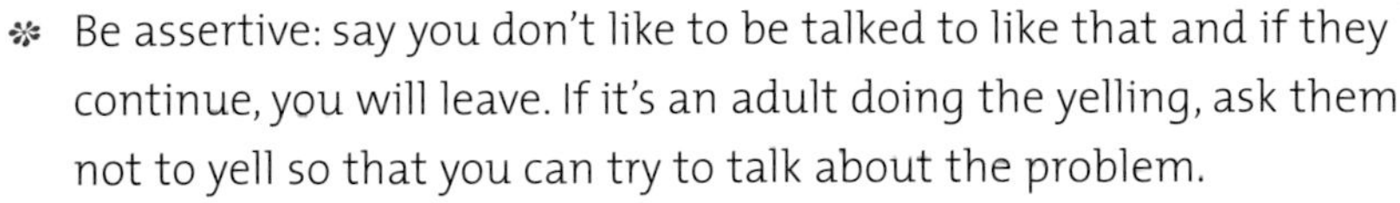

- Be assertive: say you don't like to be talked to like that and if they continue, you will leave. If it's an adult doing the yelling, ask them not to yell so that you can try to talk about the problem.
- If it doesn't look like you can resolve the problem you may need the help of a mediator (that's a neutral person who can support both sides fairly) like a parent, a teacher or another good friend.
- What's that I hear you say?? You're the culprit! There's help for you. If you think you're about to flip your lid about something, stop. Take a few deep breaths. Slow yourself down by counting to 10. Walk away from the situation that's making you angry. Take time out, like going for a walk. Yelling and swearing will only create bad feeling and if you react this way a lot, people tend to switch off. Perhaps you've been hurt about something? Try talking about your feelings clearly and explain what would make a difference for you.

THE PLASTIC-SARCASTIC

What she says can seem harmless enough—it's how she says it that can get you in the guts. When she's pulled up on her behaviour, she might try to deny it and make out that she was only joking.

What to do?

- Ignore it if you can or respond as directly as possible.
- Be assertive and name the behaviour, 'I know that you say you're only joking but your sarcastic comments are nasty and they hurt me. Please stop.'
- Get a friend to support you in this. It's always great when a friend helps you in times like these.

IS IT A SIN TO FIGHT WITH OUR GAL PALS?

Close buddies can have an unspoken rule that you must agree on everything, always be supportive and never be irritated by each other. Also, this can sometimes mean that you're expected to say and do things that they want you to do, instead of going with your own feelings! This can be a little unreasonable and if they try to pressure you into doing things you don't want to do this is when it becomes peer pressure. Can you relate to this?

A friend once told me that she never really trusted anyone until she'd had a fight with them. While I don't suggest you get out there and roll up your sleeves, I think what my friend meant was that she liked to see all parts of a person. Their sunshiny, playful loving parts as well as their grumpy troll parts.

Working on a conflict can be a great time to take a closer look at yourself, your attitudes and beliefs. If worked on positively, conflicts can deepen understanding between friends and family and can actually strengthen those relationships.

This next bit of advice can be hard to do but it's worth it. If you feel some tension with a close friend or family member ask them to tell you what they really love about you and also what they could live without. Tell them to be truthful but sensitive. Listen to what they say and take it to heart; this is how others see you. Make a promise to strengthen your good points and work on the more challenging ones.

And just because your friends are doing or saying something, doesn't mean you have to as well! Especially if it's something that hurts another person or if you disagree with it. Think about what it is that's important to you and try to stay true to yourself.

Learning to listen to your feelings during puberty is an important first step in growing up and adulthood. Honouring your feelings is an important part of having your feelings respected by others.

Check out your conflict-resolving muscles

KEEP IT CLEAN!

No, it's not about brushing your teeth and taking a shower before you have a conflict! It's about making a difficult talk go much better than you feared.

- When you want to tell someone how you see things, don't criticise them or put them down, otherwise they won't listen and you might make the problem worse.
- Keep your complaints short and to the point. If you list a thousand past hurts, you might find the other person getting irritated or just switching off.
- Be assertive—which means, say it like you mean it! Your tone of voice, facial expression and body posture need to match your words. It might feel a little strange to use a serious tone but it's all part of taking yourself seriously and getting your point across. So try it and be brave. A good tip is that even if you don't feel it, act it. Hold your head up and stand with pride.
- Avoid saying, 'It's not fair'. This is a way of blaming the other person rather than taking responsibility for what you want. Instead, talk about what options there are and what you're prepared to do.
- Avoid begging (you know what I mean, 'Oh, please, please, plllease can I have the . . . Nintendo???). Apart from being majorly annoying to anyone within earshot it doesn't usually get you anywhere. Try stating clearly and briefly what it is you want and the reasons you want it. Your parents or teacher may be shocked enough to give it to you! If it doesn't work out then take a deep breath and drop it. Think about it, acceptance helps strengthen dignity.

Love that you're a loser!!
In the world of conflict you win some and you lose some! It all evens out in the giant universal washing machine! Losing doesn't make you any less of a person. In fact, it takes major guts to admit you're wrong, to back down or to give in every now and then.

YOU KNOW THAT YOU'RE ON THE RIGHT TRACK WHEN:

- You start to really listen to the other person. You let them finish what they say without interrupting them with your answer or opinion or trying to defend your position.

Switch on your inner radar and monitor yourself

Close your eyes, put your hands on your belly and take a few slow, deep breaths. Take a moment to consider your deepest wish for working on and resolving the conflict. For example, do you want to clear the air about a misunderstanding? Would you like better communication and a better relationship with the other person? Or do you just want to win over your point of view?

- You feel you have clearly stated what your take is on things or what you need without putting the other person down.
- You feel you really understand each other's views.
- You acknowledge there's some truth in the things the other person says and you take responsibility for your part in things.
- You pause, take breaths before you speak and make eye contact.
- You really honestly start to feel compassion for the other person. You show in your words, tone of voice, facial expression and body posture that you care about their feelings.
- You find yourself smiling or laughing in the middle of your discussion. Sometimes we get sooo cross and so fixed about being right that we can catch ourselves sounding ridiculous about it. Laughter can be a sign of loosening up a little, feeling lighter.
- You feel like you're chilling out. There's less tension in your throat and face. You've lowered your voice, you feel softer around your eyes, mouth and jaw.

BUT REMEMBER, THINGS MIGHT START TO GO DOWN THE DRAIN IF:

- You start to yell and you feel that you just want to win the argument.
- You won't let the other person finish their sentences without interrupting.
- You both keep going around and around in circles and neither person is giving a little.
- You start to name call, tease, swear, use sarcasm or threaten the other person.
- You blame the other person for everything that's gone wrong.
- You start to stonewall—that's like switching off when they speak, looking away, rolling your eyes in the air and all that stuff which can be so annoying when it happens to you.
- Everything in your body feels clenched—your face, shoulders, stomach, jaw and hands—or you feel hopeless, have a tummy ache or start to feel sick.

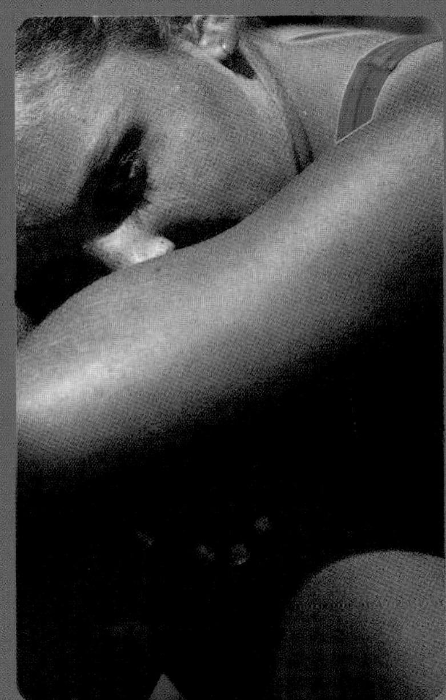

Bullying

Bullying is when someone tries to intimidate, scare or hurt you either verbally or physically. They can do this in the playground, in class or on the way home from school. They can do it in different ways like teasing, picking on you and sometimes picking a fight. And they don't always do it alone—sometimes a group of people bully one person or a group bullies another group.

What you need to know, Puberty Girls, is that bullying is not on! Whether it's you or a friend or a sister or brother who is being bullied, or whether it's someone you know who is doing the bullying, this behaviour is NOT ACCEPTABLE and it needs to stop. How do you get it to stop, you ask? Read on.

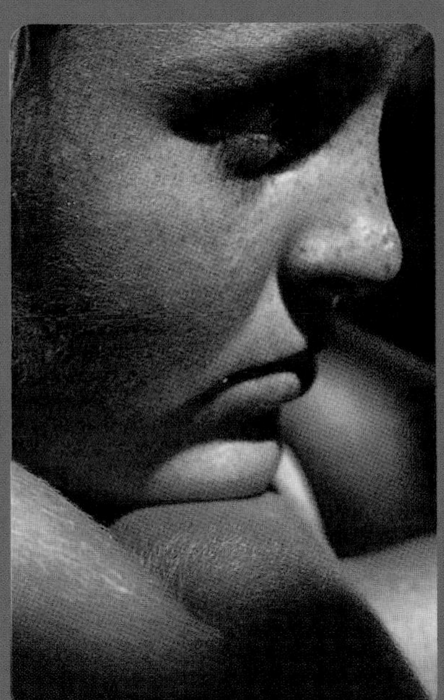

TEASING

Teasing can be personal, but a lot of the time it's not personal at all. People may zero in on some aspect about us on the outside without really knowing who we are on the inside. Like when someone teases or bullies us because we wear glasses, are overweight, are shorter or have different coloured skin. That's where teasing and bullying is absolutely ridiculous and a waste of space!

Puberty Girls out there, this is your chance to stand up for your differences and respect others. Get some of your gal pals to support you while you are doing this. The best thing that you can do is to be there for each other and stand up for each other.

HOW DO YOU DEAL WITH A BULLY?

- Hit them on the head with a sanitary pad? I don't think so! Ignore them and leave them to themselves. Try hanging out with someone else or going somewhere else. If you're in the playground choose an area closer to teachers in case the bully tries to get physical.

- Agree with them. This will shock them out of their little cotton socks! There's no real fight if there's no-one fighting on the other side. For example, if they say, 'Those glasses look really stupid on you,' you might respond with, 'Yeah they probably do' or 'I understand that's what you think' and walk away. This gives them the impression that you aren't really bothered by what they've said.
- Assert yourself. Name the behaviour, how it makes you feel and what you want done about it. Try to K.I.S.S. (keep it short and sweet) like, 'I don't like that you are putting me down, it's hurtful and I want you to stop.'
- If the verbal bullying looks like it's going to get physical, get out of there fast and get adult support straight away.
- Make sure you have supportive friends around you.

IF BAD BULLY BEHAVIOUR CONTINUES . . .

- Tell someone about it. Remember, **telling** is the first step to putting a stop to anything bad that's happening to you or a friend. Talk to your teacher, your parents or school counsellor and get help. A bully might not hear 'stop' from you but they might pay more attention when it comes from an adult.
- If you're at school, tell a teacher and play near a teacher. This is a good way of keeping safe.
- Report the problem to your school principal—talk to them or write them a letter or do both.
- When you're out of school walk with your friends, especially if you think you might bump into the bully. Have a friend and be a friend, so that you're supporting each other.
- If your friends are away or not available, or if you think the bully might hurt both you and your friend, then get an adult's help. Tell them that you need someone to walk with you.

The final word on resolving conflict

Take a moment to reflect on what you've read so far ... most of the time, conflict is about a misunderstanding or seeing things in different or opposite points of view. So trying to put yourself in another person's shoes is a good way of seeing their point of view and how they feel. And of course, remembering to treat people with respect and asking them to treat you with respect is the best way to avoid conflict.

Keep on shining Puberty Girl!

chapter 9

Puberty Girl takes on the WORLD

So you've noticed that you're changing...

But guess what? You're not the only one! If you take a look around, you'll see that someone in your family, school and circle of friends is going through similar or even the same stuff! For starters, all your girlfriends and boyfriends are going through changes themselves and are probably feeling just as confused, embarrassed, excited and curious as you. In fact it's usually a time when you're all checking each other out. Who's started to get boobs, whose voice is cracking, who's got a family of pimples growing on their chin and which boy's shoulders are looking broader? While you're looking around you might also find yourself checking out the eye candy. Those annoying boys in years 3 and 4 are starting to look a little sweeter on the eyes by the time you're in years 5 and 6. That's right, you're starting to see them as potential boyfriend material, not just annoying pests!

HEY GOOD LOOKING!

Who we dream about, think is too cute for words or have a crush on will be as different as we are. That's what makes us such a gorgeous and diverse bunch. Just as some of us may like taller, shorter, dark-haired, curly-haired, muscly, thin, quiet types, talkative types, thoughtful book types or out-there sporty types, gender is also one of these choices. We can be attracted to guys or girls or both. These choices are all part of growing up and finding out who you are. There are no right or wrong paths or rules for this. It's whatever is best for you and it involves learning about who you are and trusting your feelings.

GAY AND STRAIGHT CAN BOTH MEAN HAPPY

Feeling romantic about a person from the opposite sex is described as **heterosexuality**. (It comes from the ancient Greek word **heteros,** meaning other.) For those of us who may be more romantically interested in a person from the same sex, the word for this is **homosexuality** (another ancient Greek word, **homos**, which means same). You've probably heard the more common words 'gay' or 'lesbian' (a homosexual female) to describe homosexuality and 'straight' for heterosexuality. Some people will make a choice as they get older but for others being straight or gay is something they've kind of known about themselves since they were kids.

Lots of girls in my groups have spoken about their mum being in a relationship with another woman or their dad being gay. These girls know how normal it is for their parents to be in these relationships. Everything else is the same for their parents: they study, go to work, make a home, have friends, love their children and are in love whether they're heterosexual, homosexual or **bisexual**. (**Bi** means two. People who are bi are attracted to both sexes. As someone once said, bisexual means you've got two chances of getting a date.)

But you should know that most people have had homosexual feelings, thoughts, dreams or fantasies at some point in their lives. It doesn't necessarily mean that they are homosexual. It's normal to be curious and to explore relationship choices as we develop sexually. Sometimes people have homosexual crushes or feelings but feel confused or scared by these feelings. Often this is because they've been told that it's not okay or normal to be homosexual. Whatever your sexual preference, what's most important is loving yourself and feeling proud of who you are.

'I don't want to leave my childhood because it's so much fun. Your parents make all the decisions for you so you don't have to think.' Ginnie, 10

What happens to the Puberty Boys???

If you're thinking that it's really unfair that you have to go through all these changes at puberty it might put a little smile on your face to know that the boys are going through a few of their own amazing changes! Here's a little sneak look behind the curtain at Puberty Boy!

- His penis and testicles will grow.
- Pubic hair will grow around his penis and testicles and underarms. His arms and legs will generally get hairier. And there's more! He'll get some facial hair and possibly chest hair, back and bottom hair.
- He'll have erections—some people call these 'woody', 'hard on' or 'stiffy'. That's when the tissue inside the penis fills up with blood and swells and makes the penis hard and it sticks out.
- He'll have wet dreams—the medical term is **nocturnal emissions** ('nocturnal' means happening at night and 'emission' means sending out). Wet dreams happen during sleep when a boy is having a sexy dream and ejaculates or spurts out some **semen** from his penis (semen is the liquid that carries the male sex cells known as **sperm**). No fun having to get up in the middle of the night to change your sheets.
- He'll get more hair and maybe some B.O. (body odour) around the armpits.
- His voice will change: it might be all over the place—up and down—and then it will get deeper.
- He might get some pimples/acne—on the whole, boys get it worse than girls.
- He'll grow taller and his muscles will also develop.
- His shoulders will get wider.
- Some boys (up to 60 per cent) will get some growth of breast tissue under the nipple. Like girls they may notice soreness and tenderness around the breast area. These usually go at the end of puberty.

MY GIRLFRIENDS ARE SOOO COOL!

We girls are lucky in that many of us share a close and caring relationship with our girlfriends. We feel more comfortable holding hands, sharing our thoughts and feelings, kissing and cuddling with our girlfriends than guys do. Our gal pals are precious and if we treat each other with kindness and respect then our friendships tend to grow and deepen right through to adulthood. Some girlfriends have known each other since they were in preschool. Maybe you've got friends like that.

One problem that can come up between girlfriends is gossiping. It can cause a lot of heartache and even the closest girlfriends might fall out because of it. You know the scenario: something personal is shared with a friend who then goes off and blabs it to everyone. Okay, let's suppose you're the one who blabbed—if you backtrack to when you first told someone else, it probably didn't feel right at the time. It might have felt like you'd gone against your own feelings. What if you're the one being sweet-talked into sharing your innermost secrets? Girls will often ask me: how do you know who to trust? And you know what the answer to that is? You've got to learn to trust yourself and how you feel. Let's do it now. Think back to the last time you might have got stung by gossip. Did you feel pushed to share or did you share because you wanted to be nice or to be liked? You may have noticed feelings of discomfort inside your body even while you were sharing. This might be like a fluttering or tightness in your tummy, your breathing may feel shallow or your throat might start to tighten up. These are often signs that it's not okay to share. Trust these feelings. They won't lie to you even if your friend is begging, pretty please with honey and sugar they promise they won't tell. Be true to yourself. On the flip side, if you know what it's like to be pushed into something you're not comfortable about then make sure you know how to keep a secret and don't push if a person doesn't want to share. Give your friends the respect and space that you want for yourself. You all deserve it!

PUBERTY, IT'S A FAMILY EXPERIENCE

Your relationship with your parents, brothers and sisters will definitely be changing as you're changing. You're at an age where you still need your parents but may be going out with friends more, you want to make your own decisions and generally become more independent. You may have differences of opinion, feel that you want to choose your own clothes, the sort of friends you hang out with and your hobbies. (If all of this happens as smooth as butter then, 'Hello! What is your secret? And we'll definitely have what you're having!')

The physical and emotional stuff seems to go hand-in-hand; for example, as you start to grow and develop breasts and body hair you may also start feeling shy about your body and want more privacy. You might want to talk less about what's going on for you partly because you feel more private and partly because you may not really be sure yourself. This is where parents can be really great if you let them. If you want your parents to trust you then a good start is to trust them with what's going on for you. If you feel weird talking about puberty stuff it might help to remember that your mum, grandma, great-grandma and great-great-grandma all went through puberty and all had times when they wanted to keep their bedroom door shut, didn't like the new top their mum bought them, were embarrassed about breasts, thought the boy next door was cute and had to change their period pads. You might want to start by asking them how it was for them when they got their periods, whether they told their parents and how it was handled. Sometimes mums and dads like to celebrate the coming of your first period. Hello? Celebrate?? I know, I know, you're trying to keep a lid on things and I'm talking about announcements.

It will be different for every Puberty Girl but this is an incredible time of change in your life and some of the people closest to you might like to help you celebrate puberty and celebrate you—you beautiful, talented, luscious Puberty Girl!

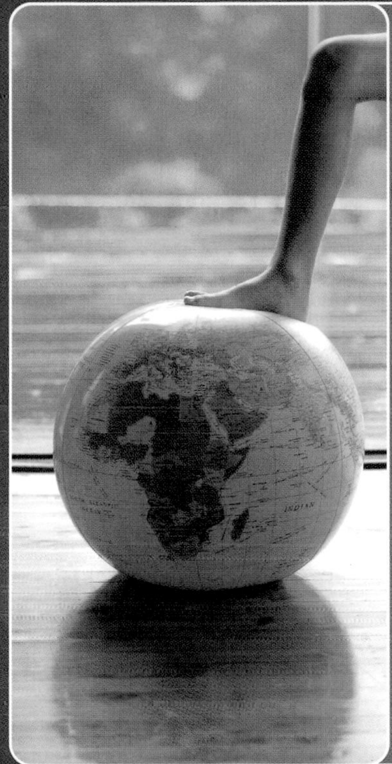

Puberty Girl meets the World!

Well, the show is nearly over, what else can I say, but good luck on your journey. Hopefully this book has helped you feel a little more chilled out about all the changes that are heading your way over the next few years, from pimples and tampons to breasts, B.O. and much more. If you've got any other questions then please write me a note. I'd love to hear how you're going. The rest is up to you Puberty Girl. With the ending of this book I pass on to you the puberty torch of glory and the honorary period pads of hope and courage (with wings of course!). You and your friends are all leaders and ambassadors in reminding girls that puberty is not a dirty word and menstruation is a healthy, normal part of growing up. You and girls all over the world, of all shapes, sizes and colours are all going through this same wonderful, crazy, mixed up journey together, and hopefully by the end of this book you are smiling, knowing with calm certainty that you are gorgeous, powerful, creative Puberty Girls! You can do anything if you put your mind to it, even get through puberty!

Who to call or contact with questions

I've prepared a list of people and places on the Puberty Girl website for you to contact if you have questions about anything, need to talk to someone or you just want to share. If you want to contact me, you can. Just log on to our website at www.allenandunwin.com/puberty.asp or email me directly on shushann@bigpond.net.au.

GLOSSARY

Adolescence (add-ul-ESS-ence)
The period of life from puberty to adulthood when a young person 'grows up'.

Anorexia nervosa
This is where a person starves themselves by eating nothing or only very little. They often do too much exercise as well so that they can control body fat and weight.

Areola (ari-OLA)
The darker circular area around the nipples.

Binge-eating disorder
This is when a person can't control their desire to overeat and often keeps the overeating a secret. Unlike bulimia (*see* Bulimia nervosa), with binge-eating disorder, a person does not vomit their food.

Bulimia nervosa
This is where a person eats a large amount of food all at once (binge eating or bingeing) and then makes themselves vomit. They might also take laxatives or diuretics.

Clitoris (CLIT-or-is)
The tiny pea-sized organ that is at the front of the vulva (*see* Vulva). It's very sensitive when directly or indirectly touched or pressed. It is a woman's organ of sexual pleasure.

Dysmenorrhea (dis-MEN-or-REE-a)
Crampy pain or discomfort at the start of and during menstruation.

Eating disorders
This is when a person has a problem with the way they eat—they either don't eat enough or starve themselves (*see* Anorexia) or they eat too much (*see* Binge-eating disorder) or make themselves throw up (*see* Bulimia nervosa).

Fallopian tubes (fa-LO-pee-in)
Two slender tubes one on either side of the uterus with really fine hairs inside that carry the egg (ovum) from the ovary to the uterus (*see* Uterus).

Genitals (jen-i-tals)
This refers to the sexual organs of either a female (the labia, clitoris, vagina) or a male (penis, testicles).

Hormone (HOR-moan)
Hormones are natural body chemicals, such as oestrogen and progesterone, that affect or control parts of the body.

Hymen (HIGH-men)
Skin that covers part of the entrance of the vagina.

Labia majora (LAY-bee-ya ma-JAW-ra meaning big lips)
The soft folds of skin that cover and protect the vagina.

Labia minora (LAY-bee-ya MY-nora meaning little lips)
Delicate skin surrounding the inner parts of the vulva that keep the vaginal opening moist. These join and protect the clitoris. They also become stimulated and swell during masturbation.

Masturbation
Touching oneself around the genitals to get sexual pleasure.

Menarche (MEN-r-kee)
A girl's first period. This usually starts between the ages of 8 to 16 years.

Menopause (MEN-o-pawz)
The last menstrual period or end of menstruation. All women can expect this to happen from age 45 to 55 years but there are some unusual cases where women have started menopause as young as 30. After menopause, a woman can no longer become pregnant.

Menstruation (MENS-troo-AY-shun)
The monthly period or menstrual bleeding. During menstruation, the extra blood and tissue that builds up inside the uterus during the menstrual cycle is expelled through the vagina, usually over a period of 3 to 7 days. Menstruation is called a 'period' because the cycle is usually over a 'period' of around 28 days.

Mucus (Mew-cuss)
A clear (or slightly yellowish), slippery fluid that helps to keep the vagina clean and moisturised.

Oestrogen (EAST-tro-jin)
A female hormone produced by the ovaries.

Ovaries (O-var-eez)
These are two organs (about the size of an almond or a small strawberry), one on each side of the uterus, in the pelvis of a female. The ovaries contain eggs (ova) and make female hormones. An ovum is one egg.

Ovulation (Ov-yule-ation)
This is when one of the ovaries releases an egg each month as part of the menstrual cycle.

Period (*see* Menstruation)

Period pain
Pain or discomfort during ovulation (*see* Ovulation). Girls and women can feel a slight ache in the side the egg is being released. It can also refer to crampy pain in the abdomen and lower back during the first and second days of your period.

Progesterone (PRO-jest-er-oan)
A female sex hormone produced by the ovaries that causes changes in the lining of the uterus.

Prostaglandin (PROST-a- gland-in)
These are hormones or chemical messengers in the blood that cause the muscular uterine wall to contract during menstruation.

Puberty (PYOO-bur-tee)
The stage of development when a child begins to grow from a child to a sexually mature person. After the changes of puberty, a person becomes capable of having children. In a girl, puberty includes a growth spurt, development of breasts and hips, growth of body hair and the beginning of menstruation (*see* Menstruation).

Pubic hair (PYOO-bik)
Thick, curly hair covering the genital area (*see* Genitals).

Reproductive organs (ree-pro-DUCK-tiv)
The parts of the body involved in reproduction (producing a baby). In a female, they include the uterus, ovaries, Fallopian tubes and vagina.

Self-esteem
This is a general term for how you feel about yourself: how you feel about who you are, the way you act and how you look. When a person doesn't like themselves very much they are said to have a low self-esteem.

Testosterone (Test-OS-ter-oan)
The male sexual hormone produced in the testes that causes male sexual characteristics to develop and increases sex drive. Girls have a smaller amount of testosterone than boys as well as the female hormones oestrogen and progesterone.

Uterus (YOO-ter-us)
This is also called the womb. The uterus is a hollow organ about the size of your fist. It sits inside your pelvis and is where a baby develops during pregnancy. The uterus is made up of muscle with an inside lining called the endometrium. The endometrium builds up and thickens during the menstrual cycle to prepare for a possible pregnancy each month. But if no pregnancy occurs, the extra tissue and blood are shed during menstruation.

Vagina (vah-JYE-na)
Sometimes called the birth canal. The vagina is a muscular passage that leads down from the cervix (the lower part of the uterus) to the outside of a female's body. During menstruation, menstrual blood flows from the uterus through the cervix and out of the body through the vagina.

Vulva
The region of the external genital organs, including the mons pubis, big outer lips (labia majora), little inner lips (labia minora), clitoris and vaginal opening.

INDEX